This series offers the concerned reader basic guidelines
and *practical* applications of religion for today's world.
Although decidedly Christian in focus and emphasis, the
series embraces all denominations and modes of
Bible-based belief relevant to our lives today. All volumes
in the Steeple series are originals, freshly written to
provide a fresh perspective on current—and yet
timeless—human dilemmas. This is a series for our times.

BOOKS IN THE SERIES:

Woman in Despair:
A Christian Guide to Self-Repair
Elizabeth Rice Handford

How to Read the Bible
James Fischer

Bible Solutions to Problems of Daily Living
James W. Steele

In the World but Not of It:
A Guide to Spirituality in Your Life
Stuart B. Litvak and Nora Burba

A Book of Devotions for Today's Woman
Frances Carroll

With God on Your Side: A Guide to Finding
Self-Worth through Total Faith
Douglas Manning

Help in Ages Past, Hope for Years to Come:
Daily Devotions from the Old Testament
Robert L. Cate

Elizabeth Rice Handford, editor of *The Joyful Woman* magazine and the wife of a pastor, has a profound grasp of the Bible principles that can make a woman successful in every area of her life —including her roles in the church, at home, and in the everyday world. She has written many books on the subject of women and religion, as well as children's stories.

Elizabeth
Rice Handford

WOMAN IN DESPAIR

A Christian Guide
to Self-Repair

Prentice-Hall, Inc., Englewood Cliffs, New Jersey 07632

Library of Congress Cataloging in Publication Data

Handford, Elizabeth Rice.
  Woman in despair.

  (Steeple books)
  Includes index.
  1. Women—Religious life.   I. Title.   II. Series.
BV4527.H37 1983   248.8'43   82-23003
ISBN 0-13-961797-3
ISBN 0-13-961789-2 (pbk.)

This book is available at a special discount when ordered
in bulk quantities. Contact Prentice-Hall, Inc., General
Publishing Division, Special Sales, Englewood Cliffs, N. J. 07632.

1   2   3   4   5   6   7   8   9   10

ISBN 0-13-961797-3

ISBN 0-13-961789-2 {PBK.}

Editorial/production supervision by Peter Jordan
Cover design by Hal Siegel
Manufacturing buyer: Christine Johnston

Prentice-Hall International, Inc., *London*
Prentice-Hall of Australia Pty. Limited, *Sydney*
Prentice-Hall Canada Inc., *Toronto*
Prentice-Hall of India Private Limited, *New Delhi*
Prentice-Hall of Japan, Inc., *Tokyo*
Prentice-Hall of Southeast Asia Pte. Ltd., *Singapore*
Whitehall Books Limited, *Wellington, New Zealand*
Editora Prentice-Hall do Brasil Ltda., *Rio de Janeiro*

Contents

Preface

Thelma was only forty years old when her husband died. In her grief she started drinking. For fifteen years she has stayed drunk, sacrificing her home, her children, and her reputation in order to get another drink. *Will God give her another chance?*

Eunice had been unhappily married for several years when she had an affair with a business colleague. A child was born as a result of the liaison. Eunice's husband knows the little girl is not his, and her presence in the home is a constant reminder of his wife's unfaithfulness. Eunice deeply regrets her sin. She loves her husband and wants to make things right with him and with God. *Is it too late?*

Phyllis is a trusted employee in a large corporation. Though she is a Christian, several years ago she began to pilfer money from her employer. Now the money she has stolen amounts to thousands of dollars. She hasn't been caught—yet—but she is tired of her sin and wants to confess it and set out to restore the money. *How can she do this without risking imprisonment and besmirching the name of Christ?*

From the time Becky was a little girl, she felt God wanted her to be a missionary. Then she fell in love with an unsaved man and married him in spite of the warnings of her father and her pastor. Now her husband doesn't even want her to go to church, yet he often leaves her alone nights to be with another woman. Becky feels her children are growing up almost as heathen as the natives across the sea she once felt called to serve. She wonders if she has made so many wrong choices that it will be impossible for God to help her. *Is it?*

This book is for women who feel they have missed God's will for their lives. If you feel you no longer deserve the name "Christian" because of the things you've done, if you long to be a good Christian but don't know how to untangle the snarls of your life, if you carry a load of guilt for things you've done, then this book is for you.

This book carries the message that God still loves you and cares about you. It affirms that you can, today, in the place where you are *right now*, do what God wants you to do. It gives you the steps, one by one, to rebuild your damaged life.

ix

But this book is also for women who have *never* claimed to be a Christian. If you know nothing about the Christian life, if you carry a terrible load of guilt for the past but don't know what you can do to change it, and if you are afraid to face a holy God, then this book is for you.

It carries the message that God loves you so much that He has already provided a way to redeem you, to pay for your sins, to cleanse you of guilt and regret, to help you live a happy, productive Christian life, and to assure you of eternal joy in Heaven. You may experience these joys if you will only accept them.

Does that sound like too much to promise?

Why not read this book and find out?

Scripture quotations are from the King James version. Scripture references are abbreviated according to the following table. The number in front of the colon refers to the chapter in that Bible book; the number following the colon refers to the number of the verse. The reference *Rom. 6:23* tells you the Scripture being quoted may be found in the book of Romans, chapter 6 and verse 23.

Genesis	Gen.	Lamentations	Lam.
Exodus	Exod.	Ezekiel	Ezek.
Leviticus	Lev.	Daniel	Dan.
Numbers	Num.	Hosea	Hos.
Deuteronomy	Deut.	Joel	Joel
Joshua	Josh.	Amos	Amos
Judges	Judg.	Obadiah	Obad.
Ruth	Ruth	Jonah	Jonah
I Samuel	I Sam.	Micha	Micah
II Samuel	II Sam.	Nahum	Nahum
I Kings	I Kings	Habakkuk	Hab.
II Kings	II Kings	Zephaniah	Zeph.
I Chronicles	I Chron.	Haggai	Hag.
II Chronicles	II Chron.	Zechariah	Zech.
Ezra	Ezra	Malachi	Mal.
Nehemiah	Nehe.	Matthew	Matt.
Esther	Esth.	Mark	Mark
Job	Job	Luke	Luke
Psalms	Ps.	John	John
Proverbs	Prov.	Acts	Acts
Ecclesiastes	Eccl.	Romans	Rom.
Song of Solomon	Song of Sol.	I Corinthians	I Cor.
Isaiah	Isa.	II Corinthians	II Cor.
Jeremiah	Jer.		

chapter one

"Nor all your tears wash out a word of it"

*"And I will restore to you
the years that the locust hath eaten."*
Joel 2:25

It was dusk. The closing session of our women's retreat had just begun. We'd spent the day talking together about the good things God has planned for Christian women and how they can be attained. One of the participants stepped up to the speaker's platform and handed me a note which read, "Libby, I've listened carefully to everything you've taught today, and I believe it's all true. How I wish I'd been taught it forty years ago. But what do you do when you are sixty-five years old, and you've already blown it?"

We start to smile when we hear that rueful admission— "I've blown it!"—but sudden pain stabs at the heart, for we've "blown it" too. Oh, perhaps we haven't blown it exactly in the same way this woman had. But it isn't necessary to be sixty-five years old to feel you've already spoiled your life. We remember the dreams we used to dream, and the present reality is shattering. We remember abrasive relationships or wrong commitments we've made, or perhaps our children are uncommunicative and rebellious, or our husbands silent and bitter.

Virginia used her husband's pistol to shoot him.[1] She'd been seeing another man. Her husband came to persuade her to come home, so she shot and killed him. "I wasn't even sorry I'd done it," she sobbed, "I'd hated him so—until I saw his mother weeping at the funeral. Then I realized what a wicked thing I'd done."

Irene had four children when she found she was pregnant again. She made up her mind she would not bear that baby, no matter what. She aborted herself. "I kept telling myself it wasn't really a baby after all. . . . But afterward, when I held that tiny form in my hands and saw its little arms and legs, I knew I'd murdered a human being—I murdered my own child!"

Janet committed adultery with her husband's best friend. Her husband was doubly wounded—betrayed by his friend, whose loyalty he'd never doubted, and by his wife, who had vowed to love him to eternity. "What do I do now? How can I ever make it right?" she asked.

Mary's days were measured by furtive drinks, and her nights were unmeasured oblivion. Her face was ravaged with the marks of sin. Her body was almost destroyed. "Have pity on me, Libby. I hate the stuff for what it does to my family, but I love it, and I can't live without it."

I've wept with them all, helped them as I could—but then at night I've sobbed out to God in agony because of the devastation sin has wrought in this lovely world. How God's loving heart must grieve at His ravished creation! Is He ever sorry He created us? Does He regret He gave us the freedom to choose, when He knew we'd choose evil instead of good?

We *have* all sinned. We have all "blown it." All the tears

---

[1]The illustrations in this book are about real people. I've used fictitious names throughout and altered some details to protect their privacy.

of regret we shed cannot change the fact of our sin nor its consequences. An ancient Persian poet said,

The Moving Finger writes; and having writ,
Moves on: nor all your Piety nor Wit

Shall lure it back to cancel half a Line
Nor all your Tears wash out a Word of it.

(The Rubyat of Omar Khayyam,
translated by Edward Fitzgerald)

The cynical poet was right. Regret, sorrow, tears—none of these change the fact that something precious has been irrevocably damaged by the choices we have made.

A girl may deeply regret her lost purity. Her regret will not give her fatherless baby a father.

A wife may weep bitter tears because she has squandered money carelessly. That will not erase the back-breaking, strength-sapping load of debt.

A woman may come to realize she is shackled by her thirst for liquor, but her addicted body will still crave it, and the damage to her body is not reversed by her regret.

What makes it hurt so much is the shattering contrast between reality and what we have dreamed. Oh, the sweet dreams of youth, the pure desires, the golden castles, the eager anticipation—how we've spoiled them and ruined them!

But, thank God, there *is* a remedy, and that's what this book is all about. There *is* a way you can have forgiveness and cleansing and a new start, *no matter how badly you've blown it.*

God wants to meet you *now,* where you are, not where you wish you were. God wants to bless you in *this* place, under the circumstances you find yourself today. Today, you can do the sweet will of God for your life.

5

Matthew 20:1-16 records a strange parable. It's almost incomprehensible to our way of thinking, until we remember that Jesus Himself told the story to teach us about the God of Heaven who always, forever, does right, even when dealing with us who've blown it. The parable begins with an ordinary business transaction. A farmer needed some day laborers to work in his vineyard. He went to the courthouse square, found a group of men waiting to be hired, contracted with them for a day's wages, and put them to work. Later in the morning, because he needed more workers, he went back to the marketplace, talked to the loiterers there, promised to pay them fairly, and put them to work. Throughout the day, he hired others. Finally, at the eleventh hour, with only an hour of daylight left to work, he went once more to the marketplace. (Oh, thank God, this husbandman-picturing God never gives up on us! He just keeps coming back, seeking us!) At that late hour, he found men standing idle in the marketplace. Why hadn't they been hired earlier? We don't know the reasons, but whatever they were, these men had wasted nearly the whole day. The precious daylight hours were irretrievably gone.

"Come work for me," he said to the idle men. "I'll pay you fairly."

These men, so long idle and unproductive, set to work for one brief, twilight hour.

Then they lined up for their wages with the other men who had toiled all day long. The husbandman paid them—oh, what grace!—a *full day's* wage.

The other workers protested. "It's not fair! We've toiled all day under the hot sun. It's not fair to pay them as much as you pay us."

"Isn't this the amount you and I agreed upon?" the master asked reasonably. "It's a fair wage. About these others

6

—it's my money. I have a right to use it as I choose, and I choose to reward these who started so late."

Awesome, gladsome fact! There is a God in Heaven who has compassion on those who have blown it. In Joel 2:25 He promised, "I will restore to you the years that the locusts have eaten." God wants to forgive you for your sin. He longs to help you rebuild the damaged relationships. He wants to give you the strength to break the bonds of evil habits. You see, He is the God of the second chance. There is a place of forgiveness and mercy even to those who have hopelessly blown it.

chapter two

What God hath in mind for you

"But God, who is rich in mercy, for his great love wherewith he loved us, Even when we were dead in sins, hath quickened us together with Christ . . . That in the ages to come he might shew the exceeding riches of his grace in his kindness toward us through Christ Jesus."
Eph. 2:4-7

If ever there were a fact that defied human comprehension, surely it is this, that the invisible, eternal Creator of Heaven and earth would incarnate Himself in a human body. God Himself stooped to become a man. The mind is boggled by the implications!

Job said, "What is man, that thou shouldest magnify him? and that thou shouldest set thine heart upon him? And that thou shouldest visit him every morning, and try him every moment?" (Job 7:17, 18). We find it incredible that this God, the great and terrible God who inhabits eternity, could long for fellowship with ordinary human beings. How could He, the One who is holiness and perfection, find joy in communing with us weak and sinning mortals? But He does! It's a mystery beyond comprehension, but it's true! God created you because He wanted to be friends with you.

Imagine the joy Adam and Eve must have experienced walking in the cool of the day in the Garden of Eden with God Himself. Think of Abraham, whom God called His friend, sitting under an oak tree, arguing with God about the destruction of Sodom. Think of Sarah, busily stirring up a batch of biscuits for the Lord of Heaven Himself to eat! And Moses, not like those other prophets who had to deal with God through an intermediary, walked into the Holy of Holies of God's presence without fear. Remember Job, whose integrity so delighted the heart of God that, of all the thousands of men living on earth, God pointed him out to Satan as one who pleased Him.

Psalm 139 tells us of the overwhelming, personal interest God has in His children. He knows our thoughts, our actions, our heart's desires. And all day long every day, He thinks of us and plans for our good. Psalm 139:17, 18 says, "How precious also are thy thoughts unto (toward) me, O God! how great is the sum of them! If I should count them, they are more in number than the sand: when I am awake, I am still with thee."

Psalm 40:5 says the same thing: "Many, O Lord my God, are thy wonderful works which thou hast done, and thy thoughts which are to us-ward: they cannot be reckoned up in order unto thee: if I would declare and speak of them, they are more than can be numbered."

God created us in His own image and then fashioned a marvelous world just for our enjoyment and challenge. He gave us the tremendous job of subduing the earth and thereby glorifying Him. God wanted each child of His to "come in the unity of the faith, and of the knowledge of the Son of God, unto a perfect man, unto the measure of the stature of the fulness of Christ" (Eph. 4:13). That was the great and good plan of God when He created us.

So what happened?

We blew it.

We spoiled it.

We ruined everything by our sin.

If you ever wanted an example of someone who blew

it, consider Eve. She lived in Paradise. She enjoyed the sweet attentiveness of a man who loved her more than life itself. She had everything her heart could desire—food, shelter, and satisfying, useful work to do. Best of all, in the evening, she could walk and talk face-to-face with God Himself.

But Eve, who had everything, coveted the one desire she didn't have. She wanted to be "like God." Like Satan, she said in her heart, "I will exalt my throne above the stars of God" (Isa. 14:13). She reached for the stars, not realizing she stood on earth, the most glittering star of God's universe, the jewel of His creation. So she listened to Satan, the enemy of her soul. She believed Satan's lie. She took of the forbidden fruit and gave it to her husband. Together they stumbled into the gloom and terror awaiting doomed sinners, and they dragged with them a ruined universe. Because they sinned, the foundations of the world were twisted out of course (Ps. 82:5). Famine, disease, floods, earthquakes, all are the bitter result of man's rejection of God and all that is holy and good. Humanity, that pinnacle of God's creation, slithered helplessly toward the yawning pit of eternal death!

... *"But God!"*

Thank God for those two words which begin Ephesians 2:4. "But God, who is rich in mercy, for his great love wherewith he loved us, Even when we were dead in sins, hath quickened us together with Christ, (by grace ye are saved;) And hath raised us up together, and made us sit together in heavenly places in Christ Jesus: That in the ages to come he might shew the exceeding riches of his grace in his kindness toward us through Christ Jesus. For by grace are ye saved through faith; and that not of yourselves: it is the gift of God" (Eph. 2:4-8).

So it was that, when Eve sinned, God *already* had a plan. He promised her, "Though you have sinned, I will give

you a seed, a Son, who will triumph over death for you."
In Genesis 3:15, God said to Satan, "I will put enmity
between thee and the woman, and between thy seed and her
seed; it shall bruise thy head, and thou shalt bruise his heel."
Eve, by faith, accepted God's promise and named her son
Seth, "Appointed One," not yet understanding that it would
be many hundreds of years before the Seed, Jesus, would be
born.

The God who made us was not taken by surprise by our
sin. It did not catch Him unawares when we rejected Him.
He offered us the choice of good or evil. We chose evil, but
God in His mercy made provision for our sin before we were
even born.

Revelation 13:8 tells us Jesus was "the Lamb slain from
the foundation of the world." The Apostle Peter told the
Jews that, even though they were the ones who crucified
Jesus, He had been delivered to them "by the determinate
counsel and foreknowledge of God" (Acts 2:23).

Long before we were born God made provision for the
fact that we would sin. Before He even created us, God the
Father covenanted with God the Son, Jesus, to save us,
because They knew we were going to blow it. Romans 5:8
tells us, "But God commendeth his love toward us, in that,
while we were yet sinners, Christ died for us."

> *Long before I knew Him, Jesus thought of me,*
> *Left His home in glory to die on Calvary;*
> *Gave His life a ransom, from sin to set me free;*
> *Long before I ever knew Him, Jesus died for me.*
>   Frances Johnston Roberts

The infinite mercy of God was extended, not just to those
who knew how wrong they'd been and were sorry for it, not
only to those who sinned in ignorance, but that mercy was

extended even to those who deliberately sinned, those who hated God, who loved their sin, and didn't want to be delivered from it.

A well-meaning Christian woman once said to a little girl, "Honey, have you found Jesus?" The little girl's eyes grew round. "Oh, no, Lady, Jesus wasn't lost. *I* was. Jesus kept looking for me until He found me."

The little girl was right. We weren't looking for Christ. We were running away from Him. "When we were yet without strength, in due time Christ died for the ungodly" (Rom. 5:6). We were ungodly, lost, and fleeing from the loving kindness of God, running as hard as we could away from Him. We shrank from Him, clinging to our filthy sins, despising His grace. But, wonder of wonders, Christ loved us, died for us, and now He pursues and woos us, begging us to accept His free gift of salvation.

This is the only hope for all of us who have blown it. Regret is vain; it cannot change what is past. The sincerest resolutions are useless; the human heart is powerless to keep them. Rituals of religion cannot erase the debt of guilt. There is no way, ever, sinners can get forgiveness for their sins by their own acts, because they have already earned their wages—hell. "The wages of sin is death" (Rom. 6:23).

That's why Jesus died on the cross—to pay for the debt we incurred by our sins. He was perfect. He never sinned. He had no debt of His own to pay. So He said, "Let me trade places with you. I'll take the penalty for your sin. I'll die in your place. You take upon yourself the reward of my righteousness. You may enter Heaven on My credit."

"The wages of sin is death," He says, *"but* the gift of God is eternal life through Jesus Christ our Lord" (Rom. 6:23).

What is required to receive forgiveness for your sin? Only two simple things: turning away from your sin (the

Bible calls that *repentance*) and turning to Christ for salvation (the Bible calls that *faith*).

Repentance is not simply feeling sorry about the results of your sin. It is agreeing with God about the wickedness of sin. We have broken God's law. Romans 7:13 tells us He gave us the law, the commandments, so we would realize how badly we had broken His laws and how exceedingly sinful our sin really is. The first step, thus, is *recognizing* your need.

The second step is asking God to forgive you because Jesus died to pay for your sin. How much faith must you have? Only enough to ask. How much repentance? Enough to want your sin forgiven and blotted out.

Receiving salvation is as tangible a transaction as the purchase of a house with the signing of a deed. It is as specific an event as the first breath and cry of a new-born baby. It is as real as the contract of marriage between a man and woman.

Because Christ loved us and died for us, we can have forgiveness for all our sins, even those we've wept over until we have no more power to weep. "The blood of Jesus Christ his Son cleanseth us from *all* sin" we are promised in I John 1:7. When we take the gift of salvation, paid for by Christ, then God forgets it forever, and so can we. God says in Hebrews 8:12, "I will be merciful to their unrighteousness, and their sins and their iniquities will I remember no more."

God promises that our sins will never be remembered again, and, what's more, "As far as the east is from the west, so far hath he removed our transgressions from us" (Ps. 103:12). A holy God says, about our forgiven sins, "I have blotted out, as a thick cloud, thy transgressions, and, as a cloud, thy sins: return unto me; for I have redeemed thee" (Isa. 44:22).

This is the basis on which you have a right to expect God to help you begin all over again.

16

chapter three

Dealing with the guilt of sin

"I acknowledge my transgressions: and my sin is ever before me. Against thee, thee only, have I sinned, and done this evil in thy sight."
Ps. 51:3, 4

Let's admit it: Christians can sin. We may not want to sin. We may hate our sin. Nevertheless, Christians can fail God. We can sin.

What is the hardest part of starting all over again? Perhaps it is finding the grace to admit we have really sinned. Something in the human heart doesn't want to say, "I've done wrong; I'm guilty."

We run to our psychoanalysts and comfort ourselves with their definitions of "false guilt." We read the latest books of self-help. All the while the Holy Spirit of God keeps probing into the dark recesses of our hearts, convicting us of failure and sin.

How we respond to His convicting Spirit, merciful in His mercilessness, determines whether or not we can make a successful new beginning. We are sorely tempted to respond the wrong way.

"I'm not so bad. There are lots of people in the world worse than I," Esther said to me. We were on a plane flying to Washington, D.C. She was a lovely foreign woman. I was hoping to be able to introduce her to Jesus, her Saviour. I told her how I had found forgiveness for my sin through Him. She said sharply, "What has a nice lady like you done that was so terrible?'

"I haven't committed murder, it's true," I answered. "But God says that if I hate someone, it's just the same as murder. I have to admit that my heart has been full of all kinds of wickedness—I just haven't let it all come out."

Her eyes filled with sudden tears. "Then I'm a murderer, too," she exclaimed. "I'm an exile from my homeland. Our president has betrayed my country and made it so I can never go home again. Sometimes I think that if I had the chance, I'd kill him."

"Then we are both sinners, aren't we?" I said gently. She nodded her shamed agreement.

We may say our sin is not very bad. But if we do, we cut ourselves off from the only remedy God offers for sin. If we deny that we are in need of forgiveness, we must suffer the intolerable consequences of our sin.

"Yes, I've sinned, but it's too late. Nothing can fix it now," Sally cried out. "Can't you see? I've ruined my home. There's no hope for me."

That's what the children of Israel answered when God told them He had seen their iniquity. They answered, "There is no hope" (Jer. 2:25). This sounded regretfully sincere, but actually it was a subterfuge to hide the fact that they liked their sin and had no intention of giving it up. No, it is never too late to give up sin. No matter what the past is, no matter how awful the sin, surely the answer is not to continue wallowing in it.

"But it's too hard to change!" you might cry. And so it would be if we were talking about some kind of self-reformation. But that's exactly what we are *not* talking about! The forgiveness for sin which the Lord Jesus offers is not made on the basis that you promise not to sin again, but rather on the basis of a debt already paid. His paying the debt is only half of His gift. He also promised to give you His Holy Spirit to live in your heart. That dear Companion, Jesus promised, will instruct you (John 14:26), guide you (John 16:13), warn you of Satan's temptations (John 14:26), and intercede with the Father on your behalf (Rom. 8:26, 27).

When you trust Christ to be your Saviour, God does not wind you up like a little mechanical doll, to make you walk a grim path alone, defenseless against the evil in your own heart. Rather, God makes you His child and promises all the resources of Heaven to help you be a successful and happy Christian.

But you must take the first step toward Him. He will not force His will upon you. He will not make you do what you do not want to do. You can have His help, but you must confess your need, and ask Him for the help He has promised.

"I can't help being what I am!" Carol said angrily. "If you knew what kind of people I came from, if you knew my inheritance, then you'd know I can't do right!"

Surely it is true that it is easier to do right when you have been trained by loving and godly parents. But God knew that when He put you in that specific home. Loving you, He gave you exactly the parents He knew you needed. He remembers what He made you of; "He knoweth our frame; he remembereth that we are dust" (Ps. 103:14). Since that is true, you can fulfill God's will for you in spite of a poor background.

You probably do experience a certain kind of temptation because of your inheritance. You may have inherited a tendency to laziness, or drunkenness, or pride, or sexual sin. (It isn't easy to tell whether the tendency is inherited or

whether a child learns from observing his or her parents.)
But if people with the same kind of inheritance you have
were ever able to succeed in spite of their inheritance, then
you too can succeed. Perhaps you've seen a boy become a
drunkard, just like his father, and say he could not help himself. But his brother, the son of the same drunken father,
hates liquor with all his heart and never touches it. So your
inheritance does not condemn you to the bondage of any
sin.

The children of Israel were troubled about this. They
said, "The fathers have eaten sour grapes, and the children's
teeth are set on edge" (Ezek. 18:2). But the Lord said, "Ye
shall not have occasion any more to use this proverb in
Israel. . . . the soul that sinneth, it shall die" (Ezek. 18:3-4).
He went on to explain that if a righteous man had a son, and
that son sinned, then the wicked son "shall surely die"
(18:13). If the son of the wicked man should see "all his
father's sins which he hath done, and considereth, and doeth
not such like, he shall not die for the iniquity of his father,
he shall surely live" (18:14-17).

Bible history shows inheritance is not what determined
whether a man did right or wrong. Godly men sometimes
bore ungodly sons. Ungodly men sometimes had godly sons.
The truth is, we all make our own choices, and we are all
accountable for those choices. We can, as Ezekiel 18:14 says,
"consider" the fruits of sin and the rewards of righteousness,
and determine to do right. You *can* decide for yourself.
God holds you accountable for *yourself*.

God will not let your background or your circumstances
keep you from doing His will for you. You may feel you have
fewer chances of succeeding spiritually because you did not
have good training. You may have very difficult circumstances—an unsaved spouse, an aggravating home situation,

an irritating fellow employee, a handicapped child, or perhaps a physical disability. Surely these are great handicaps. But those circumstances cannot keep you from doing the will of God. In spite of your home training or background and in spite of your present circumstances, God had a plan for your life today that takes those into account. You can serve the Lord today. The God who created you knows all about your limitations, and the task He has for you to do is designed with those limitations in mind.

"My substance was not hid from thee," said King David to the Lord, "when I was made in secret, and curiously wrought in the lowest parts of the earth. Thine eyes did see my substance, yet being unperfect; and in thy book all my members were written, which in continuance were fashioned, when as yet there was none of them" (Ps. 139:15, 16). God chose your background for you, *on purpose,* to make you the kind of person He needs to do His special will.

No one else can make decisions affecting you that can keep you from doing God's will. Take, for instance, the case of Amelia.

The lines around her mouth showed the bitterness she'd felt for thirty years. "I just can't forgive my husband," Amelia whispered to me.

"Why?" I asked.

"Because he took advantage of me. I was a young and innocent girl. He was a man of the world. He seduced me and led me into sin, and I was helpless against him."

"Tell me about it."

She shuddered. "My father was very strict. He forbad me to see Reuben because he was a married man. But Reuben was—oh, I don't know—so gentle and persuasive. I believed in him. When we found out I was pregnant, he divorced his wife and married me."

"And—?"

Her mouth tightened. "I can't forgive him for ruining me. That's all there is to it."

"But your father tried to stop you?"

She nodded.

"So you sneaked out to date a married man?"

She nodded.

"Then you weren't so young and innocent, were you? You knew what you were doing was sinful, didn't you?"

She closed her eyes, and a tear trickled down her cheek. "Oh, yes, God forgive me; I knew I was doing wrong."

"Then you'll have to stop putting all the blame on your husband and start taking the responsibility for your own sin, won't you?"

"Yes, yes!" she sobbed. "I see it now. I've blamed him for it all these years, and that's why I never could get it fixed, isn't it?"

As long as Amelia used her innocence as her excuse for sinning and blamed her husband, she was unable to find forgiveness for herself and unable to forgive her husband. Then she came to realize that *she* had climbed over the fences her father had set for her protection. *She* had willfully broken his rules in order to date a married man. Amelia was not accountable for her husband's sin (for surely he had gravely sinned as well); but was accountable for the wrong choices she had deliberately made and for grieving a holy God. When she came to see her own guilt and admitted it, she found true repentance and forgiveness and new hope for her marriage.

But sometimes our temptation is not to ignore our sin. Rather, we may decide our sin is too wicked to try to seek God's forgiveness. Satan doesn't care which of his traps we fall into, just as long as he keeps us from finding peace with God.

Barbara had beautiful big eyes, and they darkened with pain as she asked, "What if I have committed the unpardonable sin?" Her face bore the scars of her sin—the years she'd spent in drunkenness, hard drugs, and prostitution. She could not see how God could possibly forgive her for all she had done.

The Bible does speak of an unpardonable sin. To blaspheme the Holy Ghost, Jesus said, is not forgiven in this world or in the world to come (Matt. 12:31, 32). But we need to understand that blaspheming the Holy Ghost is not a thoughtless slip of the tongue, not just a careless curse word, not even an angry, bitter outburst against the Holy Spirit. The unpardonable sin is a continuing, conscious, implacable rejection of God's grace to the end of life. To blaspheme the Holy Spirit is to continue to reject His wooing and to spurn God's offer of salvation. The sin that is not forgivable is the sin of *not taking* God's forgiveness for sin.

"The blood of Jesus Christ his Son cleanseth us from *all* sin" (I John 1:7). "If we confess our sins, he is faithful and just to forgive us our sins, and to cleanse us from *all* unrighteousness" (I John 1:9).

Whatever wicked sin that people commit today— adultery, murder, betrayal, treason—someone in the Bible already committed it, and the Scripture tells us of their forgiveness.

In Psalm 51, King David prays for forgiveness from God. Though he was a Christian, a "man after God's own heart," he had committed adultery with the wife of one of his most loyal soldiers. Then, to cover his sin (a child had been conceived), he tricked his friend into carrying his own death warrant, and murdered him in battle. Unpardonable sins!— and yet they were pardoned by a loving, holy God through the coming death of Christ on the cross (II Sam. 12:9-14).

No wonder David said, in Psalm 103:10-14, "He hath not dealt with us after our sins; nor rewarded us according to our iniquities. For as the heaven is high above the earth, so great is his mercy toward them that fear him. As far as the east is from the west, so far hath he removed our transgressions from us. Like as a father pitieth his children, so the Lord pitieth them that fear him. For he knoweth our frame; he remembereth that we are dust."

In fact, the very passages of Scripture some use to try to prove that the line separating sin from the unpardonable sin can be casually and irretrievably crossed actually warn that it is the final rejection of salvation that dooms a person to hell. Whenever a person repents of his or her sin and turns to Christ, God is waiting to forgive. In fact, the very concern you feel about your sin is the best evidence that you have not committed the unpardonable sin.

"I thought I was saved. How could I have committed this sin and still be a child of God?" a pastor's wife asked me. Her husband had caught her setting up a tryst with a man in a hotel room.

Even Christians can commit wicked sins. Lot, the nephew of Abraham, chose to live with the wicked men of Sodom. He even callously offered his virgin daughters as decoys to divert his homosexual friends from defiling the angels whom God had sent to rescue Lot. Nevertheless, in spite of the evidence, Lot was a saved man. In II Peter 2:7,8, he is called "just Lot" and "that righteous man." Although day by day he contaminated his soul by the wickedness of Sodom, he was still a Christian: "That righteous man, dwelling among them,...vexed his righteous soul from day to day with their unlawful deeds" (II Pet. 2:8).

If your salvation depended on your ability to keep

26

yourself fit for Heaven, then, of course, when you sinned, you would lose your salvation. But God's promise of eternal life was not made to you on the condition of your promise not to sin. If you couldn't *make* yourself good enough to merit Heaven, you certainly can't *keep* yourself good enough to merit Heaven!

Nor does your eternal safety depend on the depth of your sincerity. "The heart is deceitful above all things, and desperately wicked: who can know it?" (Jer. 17:9). We are double-minded, victims of the "old" man of the heart, who still controls our behavior (Rom. 7:18-23). It is impossible for us to guarantee that we are totally sincere.

Nor does our eternal security depend on our strong faith. If we had enough faith only to ask Jesus to save us, however timidly, then Jesus saved us. The father of an afflicted child asked Jesus to heal the boy, and he said, "Lord, I believe, help thou mine unbelief" (Mark 9:24). He had a lot of unbelief, but he had enough belief simply to ask, and that was all the faith Jesus required. Jesus healed the lad in spite of a father's weak faith.

No, our salvation depends only and completely on *God's* ability to keep His promise. He said He would save you if you asked Him to. Your safety depends on the almighty power of a loving God to do what He promised He would do.

He wants to save us: all Scripture assures us of this. If we want Him to save us, would He obscure the way? If our hearts are moved to respond to His offer of salvation, would He trick us? Would He require some secret code, some magic words impossible for us to find, or some standard we could not humanly meet? That doesn't make sense! Why would God so lovingly plan, from the foundation of the world, a way to save us from hell, and then make it so complicated we couldn't find it? Why would He make our salvation dependent on our ability to "hold out faithful" when He knew we couldn't possibly "hold out"? That is not the act of a loving, reasonable God!

God says in Luke 11:13 that we human parents, weak and sinning as we are, would not do that to our children. And certainly this loving, holy God will not do that to us when we ask Him for salvation. "If a son shall ask bread of any of you that is a father, will he give him a stone? or if he ask a fish, will he for a fish give him a serpent? Or if he shall ask an egg, will he offer him a scorpion? If ye then, being evil, know how to give good gifts unto your children: how much more shall your heavenly Father give the Holy Spirit to them that ask him?" (Luke 11:11-13).

All the words in the Bible that describe this act of taking Christ as Saviour—"believe," "come," "receive," "take," "drink," "ask," "open the door"—these are not barriers to be climbed over to reach salvation, but rather are simple descriptions of the heart attitude God wants you to have. So, you may be sure, "him that cometh unto me I will *in no wise* cast out" (John 6:37).

"But surely I lost my salvation when I did this terrible thing," you might protest. Yes, you might have lost your salvation when you sinned—any sin, not just this terrible one—*if* your salvation depended on *your* works. That's why Ephesians 2:8, 9 emphasizes that it is "by grace are ye saved through faith; and that not of yourselves: it is the gift of God: Not of works, lest any man should boast."

Would this marvelous guarantee of Heaven make a born-again Christian indifferent to sin? Would this grace make us careless about sin, saying, "Since I'm going to Heaven anyway, it won't matter what I do; I'll sin and have my fun"? Oh, no, never—not when I realize what my sin cost the dear

Lord Jesus on Calvary. Not when I see the devastation sin wreaks in my life and the lives of those I love. Not when I understand how fleeting is the fun of sin, and how grindingly long the heartache of sin lasts.

David prayed, in Psalm 19:13, "Keep back thy servant also from presumptuous sins." Psalm 130:4 says, "There is forgiveness with thee, that thou mayest be feared." Repentance means viewing my sin as God views it, thus a believer fears (reverences) God more, not less.

There is such a thing as incomplete repentance. It might be described as regretting the consequences of your sin, rather than feeling genuine sorrow that you have sinned against a holy God. Hebrews 12:17 tells us this was Esau's problem. He had valued his inheritance so little, he sold it to his brother Jacob for a pot of stew. Esau bitterly regretted that he had lost his inheritance. But it seems his grief was for financial loss of the inheritance, not for the loss of the spiritual blessing.

Incomplete repentance says, "It wasn't really my fault I did wrong" and then blames inheritance, parents, or circumstances for the sin. True repentance says, "I am guilty; it is my fault, I have no excuse. I am sorry, and I ask God to forgive me for Christ's sake."

There are three simple steps to take in dealing with the guilt of sin:

1. Confess the sin to God. Acknowledge how sinful it really was. Admit it was your own fault and that you had no excuse.

2. Accept His forgiveness, based on the fact that Christ paid for your sin on Calvary. Rest in the assurance that the sin really is forgiven, just as God promised.

3. Set out today to do right, to establish the right

habits of life, to rebuild the broken relationships, and to deal patiently with the inevitable consequences of your sin.

chapter four

After the fall: starting over

"For I know the thoughts that I think toward you, saith the Lord, thoughts of peace, and not of evil, to give you an expected end. Then shall ye call upon me, and ye shall go and pray unto me, and I will hearken unto you."

Jer. 29:11, 12

God knew that we would blow it so thoroughly that we would feel hopeless ever to be able to make it right. The Israelites captured by King Nebuchadnezzar felt that way. The people had gone into terrible sin, sin too horrible to describe. They had practiced the most wicked kinds of sexual perversion. They had sacrificed their innocent babies to their obscene gods. God had sent His most faithful and earnest prophets to beg them to turn from their sin.

"The Lord God of their fathers sent to them by his messengers," says II Chronicles 36:15, 16, "rising up betimes, and sending; because he had compassion on his people, and on his dwelling place: But they mocked the messengers of God, and despised his words, and misused his prophets, until the wrath of the Lord arose against his people, *till there was no remedy.*"

There came a time in the lives of the children of Israel, because of their sin, that they *had* to go into captivity in Babylon under King Nebuchadnezzar. Nothing they could do would stop the certain, inevitable action of God: "Therefore he brought upon them the king of the Chaldees, who slew their young men with the sword in the house of their sanctuary, (there was to be no deliverance from punishment even in the very house of God!), and had no compassion upon young man or maiden, old man, or him that stooped for age: he gave them all into his hand," says II Chronicles 36:17.

So the Israelites found themselves in an alien, hostile land, far from their homes and temple, because they had sinned "until there was no remedy."

But, even under those circumstances, and in that land, God did not utterly forsake them. They *had* to go into captivity. That was inevitable. But they did *not* have to struggle on in their sin. Even in their bondage, God prepared the prophet Jeremiah to give them comfort and direction.

"Go down to the potter's house," God said one day to Jeremiah. "I want you to notice how the potter works the clay on the wheel."

So Jeremiah did. There he saw the potter sling a blob of clay onto the potter's wheel. He worked it deftly with his hands while he pumped the wheel with his foot.

"Look, Jeremiah," the Lord said, "see, there's a flaw in the pot. The vessel is marred." Perhaps bits of straw had been mixed with the clay or perhaps a bit of grit or stone. Perhaps the post was lopsided or the clay too wet to handle well. Whatever the problem, the pot in the potter's hands simply was a failure. It was no good.

"Watch, Jeremiah," the Lord said. "See what the potter does now." The potter picked up the spoiled, useless pot, rolled it into a ball again, and flung it back on the wheel. "The vessel that he made of clay was marred in the hand of the potter: so he made it again another vessel, as seemed good to the potter to make it" (Jer. 18:4).

The lesson? The Lord explained to Jeremiah. "O house of Israel, cannot I do with you as this potter? saith the Lord. Behold, as the clay is in the potter's hand, so are ye in mine hand, O house of Israel. At what instant I shall speak concerning a nation, and concerning a kingdom, to pluck up, and to pull down, and to destroy it; If that nation, against whom I have pronounced, turn from their evil, I will repent of the evil that I thought to do unto them," (Jer. 18:6-8).

So the children of Israel still had a choice, even in the middle of their punishment. They could repent, and, if they did, God would bless them again, even in bondage. Though they were in Babylon, away from home, and hostages, they could still have a normal, happy, and productive life—if only they would repent and turn from their sin.

So the Word of God through the prophet Jeremiah came to them: "Build ye houses, and dwell in them; and plant gardens, and eat the fruit of them; Take ye wives, and beget sons and daughters; and take wives for your sons, and give your daughters to husbands, that they may bear sons and daughters; that ye may be increased there, and not diminished. And seek the peace of the city whither I have caused you to be carried away captives, and pray unto the Lord for it: for in the peace thereof shall ye have peace. . . . For thus saith the Lord, That after seventy years be accomplished at Babylon I will visit you, and perform my good word toward you, in causing you to return to this place. For I know the thoughts that I think toward you, saith the Lord, thoughts of peace, and not of evil, to give you an expected end. Then shall ye call upon me, and ye shall go and pray unto me, and I will hearken unto you. And ye shall seek me and find me, when ye shall search for me with all your heart. And I will be found of you, saith the Lord: and I will turn away your captivity, and I will gather you from all the nations, and from all the places whither I have driven you, saith the Lord; and I will bring you again into the place whence I caused you to be carried away captive" (Jer. 29:5-14).

This means that *today* you too can do the perfect will of God. You may not have done right yesterday, but today you can do what God wants you to do.

Proverbs 24:16 says, "For a just man falleth seven times, and riseth up again, but the wicked shall fall into mischief." What characterizes a wicked man? When he falls into sin, he stays there. What characterizes a just and righteous man? When he falls, he gets back up and tries again. He isn't righteous because he fell, but because, when he did fall, he started over again to do right.

Psalm 37:23, 24 elaborates on this: "The steps of a good man are ordered by the Lord: and he delighteth in his way. Though he fall, he shall not be utterly cast down: for the Lord upholdeth him with his hand." Children of God are not immune to temptation. They will sin. But they do have God's promise to provide a way of escape; He will keep them from being destroyed. "There hath no temptation taken you but such as is common to man: but God is faithful, who will not suffer you to be tempted above that ye are able; but will with the temptation also make a way to escape, that ye may be able to bear it" (I Cor. 10:13). Here we are promised protection, not by our alertness, not by our righteousness, but by God's faithfulness to keep His promises.

He saved you from sin; He takes the responsibility to cleanse and protect you. In I John 1:8, Scripture says that "If we say that we have no sin, we deceive ourselves, and the truth is not in us." Sin in the life of a Christian is a fact. Falling is our habit. But God has promised protection and cleansing: "If we confess our sins, he is faithful and just to forgive us our sins, and to cleanse us from all unrighteousness" (I John 1:9).

So you have sinned. You have claimed forgiveness and cleansing. Now pick yourself up, dust yourself off, and start walking down the road again. You have fallen, but you are going to rise again, and set out to do right.

● The first step in starting over again is to get the mind washed clean by the Word of God. Sin distorts the thinking process. It warps the judgment and twists God's standards awry. So you will need to submit your mind to the Scriptures, meditate on them, memorize them, quote them aloud. You may despair of ever getting those evil thought patterns out of your mind, but by God's grace, you can.

Meditation on the Word of God not only corrects wrong thinking, it is the source of power and strength to do right. The Word of God will be your comfort when Satan assaults your soul. David prayed in Psalm 119:133, "Order my steps in thy Word; let not any iniquity have dominion over me."

Set out to read the Bible, all of it, again and again. "Man shall not live by bread alone, but by *every word* that proceedeth out of the mouth of God" (Matt. 4:4). Read it whether or not you feel you are profiting from it. Sometimes take a small passage, and read it over and over again until your thoughts are reshaped to fit it.

When you read a passage of Scripture and find something that exactly meets your heart's need that day, write it on a small card. Take it with you to read aloud from time to time. Feed on the Word of God. Let it cleanse your mind.

A friend of mine said to me, "Libby, I used to think I would never, never be able to erase from my mind all the filthy thoughts I'd had from the years I lived in sin—the old jokes, the raunchy songs—all the thought patterns from the habits of sin. And suddenly, just the other day, I realized that God *had* washed those out of my mind. They are gone. But it didn't happen until I started memorizing Scripture."

• Second, recognize the fact that you'll have to continue to cope with the consequences of your sin even after you've set out to do right. Repentance does not automatically eradicate the results of sin. Seeds from the past will continue to sprout, and you'll need to keep rooting out those sprouts—the evil effects of wrong decisions.

If you betrayed a loved one's trust, you'll have to continue to reearn that trust. If you abused a charge account, you'll have to rebuild a good credit record. If you had an accident driving while drunk, don't be hurt when a friend hesitates to loan you his or her car. Sin bears bitter fruit, and you will not like the aftertaste. But you can endure what you must while you rebuild your life and earn the respect of those you love. Don't despair when you find you must keep coping with the aftereffects of sin.

• Third, make habits work for you, not against you. If through the years, a wrong act was triggered by a certain behavior pattern, then change your life style to make it harder to do wrong.

"A three-fold cord is not quickly broken," Ecclesiastes 4:12 says. The factors that make it hard to break a bad habit are the same strengths that come when you establish a good habit. When you set out to stamp out a bad habit, determine what good habit you ought to replace it with. Don't leave an empty blank in your life that will make it easy to go back to the old way.

The man who swept and garnished the house of his mind clean, without the power of God, but by simply reforming himself, soon found his mind infested with seven times more demons (Matt. 12:44). Empty minutes have to be filled with *something*. Determine ahead of time what you are going to do when temptation assails you.

The pocket or purse that once held those cigarettes ought perhaps now hold a New Testament. When the hand reaches for a cigarette, it touches instead the Word of God, and the heart is automatically reminded of the new direction you have taken.

Have you been watching a certain suggestive television program? Don't simply quit watching it. Schedule that specific time each week to do a neglected, important task you'd enjoy, such as writing distant family members or jogging around the block.

If the temptation has been to drink yourself into oblivion over the weekend, then commit yourself, on Monday morning, to spend Friday evening in some strenuous physical activity helping Christian friends. "But put ye on the Lord Jesus Christ, and make not provision for the flesh, to fulfil the lusts thereof" (Rom. 13:14).

A man who came to know Christ as his Saviour decided to keep (in his refrigerator, if you please!) the last can of beer he hadn't drunk. "I want to show everybody how strong I am," he said. Naturally, the can of cold beer disappeared, and others soon took its place. He had made provision for the flesh, rather than getting temptation moved as far away as possible.

If you have turned from an illicit romantic attachment, then it's unwise to sit alone in a darkened room in the evening listening to sentimental love songs. You'll need to establish some vigorous and profitable new activities to replace the old.

Children in England used to play "The White Bear" game. They'd put their chairs in a circle and say, "Let's *not* think about a white bear." So they would sit silently, staring at each other, trying *not* to think about a white bear up in the Arctic, a white bear's great paw scooping up a fish; a white bear shuffling across the tundra; a white bear growling in the cold Arctic moonlight. So what does everyone think about? A white bear, of course!

So a woman who is desperately trying to lose weight ought not to keep thinking about a scrumptious hot fudge sundae (she is *not* going to eat) made with butter-pecan ice cream and topped with whipped cream, toasted pecans, and a tart cherry. Instead, she ought to focus on how much better she will feel when she doesn't have to carry around all that excess weight. Even more important, she ought to commit herself thoroughly to an important and useful project completely outside of herself so that she can forget about her body altogether.

These efforts require self-discipline, making yourself do what you ought to do, rather than sullenly doing what someone else requires of you. However, the self-disciplined life is not a rigid, compulsive, willy-nilly schedule, oblivious of other's needs. It isn't even necessarily doing the same thing at the same time every day. It is seeking the mind of God and doing today the important things that He wants you to do.

The right kind of self-discipline will not make critical and judgmental assessments of others. "Let him that thinketh he standeth take heed lest he fall" is the warning that precedes the promise of help in time of temptation in I Corinthians 10:13. So, godly self-discipline has compassion on others in their need and seeks to strengthen and comfort others, rather than expose and humiliate them. Why is it, then, that we so often pounce on those who are in the midst of a battle with Satan when we've scarcely won the same battle ourselves?

Self-discipline is not beating the self, not running in exhaustion, not trying to placate a vengeful and capricious God. It is not mindlessly setting up an impossible list of demands on the self. God is not a hard taskmaster. His yoke is easy; His burden is light. He wants you to come to Him and find rest (Matt. 11:30). Your motivation, your reason for trying to do right, is not a desperate attempt to gain God's favor. Rather, you are making a joyful commitment because God loves you, and you love Him in return.

You've heard of the little boy who brushed his hands off after his first day at school and said, "Well, I got that school business out of the way." Like him, you will have a sorry awakening coming if you think you can forever get rid of temptation. The little boy is going to have to go back to school for perhaps sixteen more years, before he gets his formal education out of the way. By then he'll realize that his education has just barely begun. So you must not expect to "arrive" in your conquest of temptation.

"There is no discharge in that war," King Solomon said in Ecclesiastes 8:8. The war against temptation never ends in this life. I cannot even assure you there will come a time you can be confident that this particular temptation, which has so shattered your life, will end. There is no state of perfection this side of Heaven that you can reach.

No matter how many months have gone by since the alcoholic took his or her last drink, he or she is still an alcoholic and must think of himself or herself as an alcoholic. This is true, not just of the sin of drunkenness, but of all other kinds of sins as well. "I am a sinner," you must remember; "I am a forgiven sinner, but I am nevertheless a sinner, so I must not allow myself that first step toward sin."

There are no short cuts to purity, no easy steps. There are no secrets, that, if you could only find them, would make the war against temptation effortless. That is why the Lord encourages us, in I Corinthians 15:58, to be "steadfast, unmoveable, always abounding in the work of the Lord." Today, you can do right. Today, you can say *no* to that temptation. Today, you can garrison your heart and mind with the Word of God, so that sin will not have dominion over you.

Being a woman has some built-in hazards that mitigate against the disciplined life. If you don't recognize them, if you don't stay reconciled to the reality of the pressure, you'll soon get discouraged and give up.

Nearly always, a woman has someone else in authority over her—a husband, a father, or a boss. She cannot always do what she thinks would be best with her time. Since God is the One who put her in subjection, God can use even that authority to *help* her conquer temptation, not to hinder her.

A woman is vulnerable to the varying emotions her hormones create during her monthly cycles. What she feels one week to be a challenge and joy may the next week turn into impossible despair. She must anticipate these ups and downs and comfort herself by remembering, "I'll feel differently about this next week."

The responsibilities of homemaking and the unexpected needs of children, which cannot be scheduled, make it difficult for a woman to keep a regular and systematic schedule. Children and crises go together. No matter what vows a woman has made to accomplish certain things on certain days, she'll have to give those up some times in order to meet the more important needs of her family.

All these aspects of living make it harder, perhaps, for a woman to live a disciplined life, but they can be used to strengthen rather than hurt her. The victorious Christian life is not a life untouched by temptation or sin. It is living in such close communion with the Lord Jesus, so saturated with the Word of God, that when sin does come, it is recognized and dealt with. The just man is not the man who never sins; he is the man who, when he falls, rises up again and keeps trying to do right.

chapter five

Setting new goals

"Now unto him that is able to keep you from falling, and to present you faultless before the presence of his glory with exceeding joy."

Jude 24

You have confessed your sin. You have started over again. You have determined that when you fall, you'll set out again to do right. You have committed yourself to living by the Word of God.

Now choose some new goals for your life. What is it you really want to do? to be? to see accomplished in the lives of those God holds you accountable for?

Find out from God what He wants you to do. Set goals for yourself. Be sure they are realistic and specific, so specific, you can write them down. Express them in concrete language, rather than in fuzzy, idealistic terms. Don't simply say, "I'm going to have victory," or "I'm going to be a better Christian." Rather, say specifically, "I'm going to church every Sunday," or "I'm going to quit talking back to my husband," or "I'm going to quit smoking."

My friend Jane often succumbs to deep depression. She'll phone and say, "Libby, I just don't have victory."

"What do you mean by 'victory,' Jane?" I ask.

"Oh, I don't know. I'm just not a very good Christian."

So we talk together, and after a while she can see that she's troubled specifically because she lost her temper with her daughter, and she needs to make it right. Or perhaps she spent the evening watching a sex-filled television movie when the house was dirty and needed cleaning. It is not until she can recognize a specific, definite problem that she can take specific, realistic steps to solve it.

In fact, it's a good idea, when you find yourself feeling vaguely guilty, to pinpoint the reason for your discomfort. Is God dealing with you about a real, specific sin? If so, look at it square in the face, fix it, and then enjoy God's smile again. It may be that your uneasy sense of guilt comes from Satan, that old accuser of the brethren. (Satan's name means "the hater," "the accuser," "the liar.") He wants to destroy you by any means, by false pride, discouragement, or distraction. He will accuse you by bringing to mind forgiven sin. Then you must recognize that it is *false* guilt you are feeling and turn again to rest in God's loving favor. Again, the key is to deal in the specific needs of your life, not in vague generalities.

Concentrate on the single, most important need in your life, rather than trying to handle everything you find wrong in your life. Remarkably, conquering a major bad habit often gives the ability to bring many other areas under control at the same time.

When you have chosen some realistic goals, then work out a system of checking up on yourself. Set aside a regular time—perhaps on Sunday afternoon—to see how well you are doing. If you are working on a damaged relationship with a son or daughter, think through your contacts that week. Were there some positive results? Was there a new freedom and openness in your relationship? Did you miss an opportunity you could have used? Is an event coming up you can use to strengthen the bond?

Get in the habit of writing down vows you make, insights that God gives you during your Bible study, and failures and lacks God reveals to you. Read them over, not only to remind you of decisions you've made, but also to call to mind God's faithfulness in dealing with you. The written record can be a great comfort, as it reveals even moderate growth in areas you might not happen to notice.

And, of course, success is any degree of growth. You might not have progressed as far as you longed to in your spiritual life, but any degree of growth is success!

Get intimately acquainted with the dear Lord Jesus. You have met Him already as your Saviour. Now learn to know Him as your older Brother and Friend. Hebrews 2:9-18 tells us that because we are human beings of flesh and blood, doomed to die, Jesus made Himself flesh and blood. Then, through His death, He could deliver us from death, and the bondage the fear of death puts us in. He made Himself "like his brethren" so He could be a merciful and faithful High Priest for us. He could pray for us. "For in that he himself hath suffered being tempted, he is able to succour them that are tempted" (Heb. 2:18). Are you assailed by the tempter? Then cry out to the Lord Jesus! He endured and conquered that very temptation! He remembers how it feels! He will pray for you and will help you overcome it.

When you ask Christ to aid you, you needn't wonder if He cares or if you matter to Him. He *does* care. "Seeing then that we have a great high priest, that is passed into the heavens, Jesus the Son of God, let us hold fast our profession. For we have not an high priest which cannot be touched with the feeling of our infirmities; but was in all points tempted like as we are, yet without sin. Let us therefore come boldly unto the throne of grace, that we may obtain mercy, and find grace to help in time of need" (Heb. 4:14-16). Because Jesus cares, you have a right to go straight into the presence of God *boldly!* to obtain help to overcome temptation.

Jesus remembers how it feels to be weak, assaulted by temptation, vulnerable to sin. He will give you mercy and grace to help you when you need it. So spend time with Him. Make Him not only your Saviour, but also your daily Companion.

My husband once led to Christ a man who had fought a lifetime battle with alcohol. He sensed that the man simply could not by himself fight the temptation to drink. So he said, "Joe, I want you to spend this week with me. Everywhere you go, I'll go too, and you'll come with me when I have to go somewhere. We'll be together all day long, all week. When you're tempted to drink, I'll be there to help you say 'no.' " They did spend the next seven days together. My husband read the Scriptures with him, prayed with him, encouraged him. Not once during the week did Joe take a drink.

"Preacher," he said with tears in his eyes at the end of the week, "I think I could make it if you'd just stay with me all the time."

"I can't do that, Joe," my husband answered gently, "but I know Someone who can."

That Someone, of course, is the Holy Spirit of God. He wants to walk with you day and night, to warn you of danger, to comfort you in trouble, and to encourage you to do right. Harassed, tempted child of God, meet your older Brother! Let Him walk the difficult road with you. Lean on His mercy and grace to help in time of need.

Remember that the promises God made to help you were not based on your ability to do right. They were made on the basis of God's faithfulness, not yours. "There hath no temptation taken you," says I Corinthians 10:13, "but such as is common to man: *but God is faithful,* who will not suffer you to be tempted above that ye are able; but will with the temptation also make a way to escape, that ye may be able to bear it." You can overcome temptation, not because you are strong, but because God is faithful, and because He always keeps His promises!

Now try to visualize yourself living the kind of joyful, useful life God had in mind for you when He saved you. Try to imagine what joy it will be to live in daily and hourly fellowship with the Lord Jesus. Think how, living the Spirit-filled life, you'll have the grace to respond quietly even under pressure. Visualize waking up in the morning, absolutely free to do what you really want to do, undriven by the compulsions of bad habits. "Eye hath not seen, nor ear heard, neither have entered into the heart of man, the things which God hath prepared for them that love him," says I Corinthians 2:9. You don't have an imagination good enough to even guess at how wonderful and joyful the Christian life can be, God says. But there is a way you can find out: in the Word of God. "But God hath revealed them unto us by his Spirit: for the Spirit searcheth all things, yea, the deep things of God" (I Cor. 2:10).

God has a wonderful plan in mind for you. He intends to make you a perfect person, like the Lord Jesus Himself. And today is the day He wants to begin it in you!

chapter six

Normal
(not average)
Christian living

"But the God of all grace, who hath called us unto his eternal glory by Christ Jesus, after that ye have suffered a while, make you perfect, stablish, strenghten, settle you."

I Pet. 5:10

God wants your Christian life to be filled with joy. He wants you to have daily victory over sin and enjoy constant communion with the Lord Jesus.

There are several indispensable elements in the successful Christian woman's life. First, you need daily, intimate contact with God. This means setting aside a certain amount of time every day to read your Bible (so God can speak to you) and to pray (so you can express your love and your needs to Him). It is better to take only ten minutes a day, faithfully, rather than to hope for an hour with Him every day, and end up spending no time at all. So, in the beginning, why not set aside ten minutes for the Lord to be used without fail?

I suggest you plan to read all the way through the Bible every year. We've printed a Bible-reading schedule in the back of this book as a guide for your reading (see Appendix I). You might read the New Testament passage the very first thing in the morning. (Usually this will not take you more than five minutes.) Ask the Lord to open your heart to it, to see what He wants you to change in your life, and to help you understand what He wants to reveal of Himself. Then pray, asking for wisdom and strength for the day and guidance to make the right choices.

Some time later in the day, perhaps in the evening when you have more time, read the Old Testament passage. Usually this will not take more than fifteen minutes. This would be the time to write down specific prayer requests, to set goals, to examine your heart, and to confess whatever sin you find there. Listen as you read, and plan to change your behavior to match what the Word of God requires.

The Word of God will convict you of sin: "Wherewithal shall a young man cleanse his way? by taking heed thereto according to thy word" (Ps. 119:9). The Word will protect you from temptation: "With my whole heart have I sought thee: O let me not wander from thy commandments. Thy word have I hid in mine heart, that I might not sin against thee" (Ps. 119:11). The Word will give you joy: "I have rejoiced in the way of thy testimonies, as much as in all riches" (Ps. 119:14). It explains God's dealings with you: "I know, O Lord, that thy judgments are right and that thou in faithfulness hast afflicted me" (Ps. 119:75). The Word will give you guidance: "Thy word is a lamp unto my feet, and a light unto my path" (Ps. 119:105). It reveals God's good plans for you: "Thou are good, and doest good; teach me thy statutes" (Ps. 119:68). How absolutely vital it is, for happy and successful Christian living, that you saturate your life with the Word of God!

Second, learn how to pray for specific needs and to get your prayers answered. Romans 8:32 says, "He that spared not his own Son, but delivered him up for us all, how shall he not with him also freely give us all things?" Your Heavenly

Father loved you so very much, He gave the one gift that cost Him that which was dearest to Him—His own Son. If He willingly gave you Jesus, then He will gladly give you anything else you ask. He is able, Ephesians 3:20 says, to "do exceeding abundantly above all that we *ask or think,* according to the power that worketh in us." The holy God, who created you in love, now wants you to come to Him with your needs and desires exactly as a child would come to its Daddy, confident that Daddy would *want* to do whatever is asked! Such an intimate and receiving relationship might seem foreign to the experience of the average Christian. But it should be the normal expectation of every Christian to ask "and receive, that your joy may be full" (John 16:24).

Third, memorize Scripture according to some plan, however simple. Perhaps it ought to be, at first, just one verse a week, reviewing each day the Scriptures you have already learned. In Appendix II at the back of this book are a number of Bible verses every woman ought to have stored away in her heart. Or you might copy, on a 3 X 5 index card, a verse that God lays on your heart from your Bible reading from day to day. Carry the card with you and review it while you drive, while you wait for someone, while you iron, or while you take a bath. Use those idle moments when your mind is "out of gear"; make them profitable by having Scripture at hand to memorize.

Satan, the enemy of your soul, is going to try his best to rob you of the joy of serving God. Your best defense is the Bible hidden in your heart, kept ready to use against him.

Fourth, find a fundamental, evangelistic, soul-winning, Bible-teaching church. Commit yourself to the leadership of a good pastor. It is possible for a Christian to grow spiritually without fellowshipping with other Christians and without getting strong Bible teaching. But it is not easy. So the

Lord tells His children not to forsake assembling with other Christians (Heb. 10:25).

You need contact with people who love the Lord, who are trying to do right, who are studying the Scriptures. They will encourage you when you get discouraged. They'll hold you up in prayer and lovingly warn you when your heart is getting cold toward the things of God. You need fellowship with others who also love Christ.

If a church does not believe the Bible is the actual Word of God, without error, then it will not reverence the Bible nor teach it as you need to be taught. So you need to find a "fundamental" church, one which teaches the inspiration of the Bible, the deity of Christ, His death and resurrection for the forgiveness of sins, and the need for salvation.

Be a faithful church member. Try not to miss a single public service. (One woman in our church described the Wednesday evening prayer service as the "pole that holds up the sagging clothes line in the middle of the week"! She needed it!)

Find your niche of service. Be dependable in it. Many a time, when temptation assaults you, you'll be protected simply because you are so busy doing what God told you to do, you won't have time to dally!

Christians in the early church at Jerusalem gathered together every single day (Acts 2:46). Frequent, faithful attendance at a Bible-believing church is a great strengthening influence toward a normal Christian life.

Fifth, make a public confession of your faith in Christ and get baptized. Romans 10:9, 10 says, "If thou shalt confess with thy mouth the Lord Jesus, and shalt believe in thine heart that God hath raised him from the dead, thou shalt be saved. For with the heart man believeth unto righteousness; and with the mouth confession is made unto salvation."

What happens in the heart ought to rise to the lips in a song of thankful praise!

It is hard to be a "secret believer" and have assurance that you are really saved. As we said earlier, your *salvation* depends not on how you act, because you can't do anything to make yourself good enough for Heaven. It does not depend on how you feel, but on your taking the gift of salvation. It rests on God's ability to keep His promise to save you. Your *assurance* of salvation, likewise, comes not from how you feel, but from the Word of God. Again, you know you are a child of God, not because of the way you act, but simply because God wrote the record down in the Bible. I John 5:1-13 says, "He that believeth on the Son of God hath the witness in himself: he that believeth not God hath made him a liar; because he believeth not the record that God gave of his Son. And this is the record, that God hath given to us eternal life, and this life is in his Son. He that hath the Son hath life; and he that hath not the Son of God hath not life. These things have I written unto you that believe on the name of the Son of God; that ye may know that ye have eternal life, and that ye may believe on the name of the Son of God." You can know you have been forgiven for all your sins, not by how you feel, not by how you act, but simply by the authority of the written record, God's Word.

If you doubt that Jesus saved you when you asked Him to save you, whom are you calling a liar? In John 5:10, God says you call Him a liar if you doubt Him. Is it presumptuous to say, "I know I am going to Heaven, because Jesus forgave me"? Oh, no! On the contrary, it is calling God a liar to say, "I *hope* I'm going to Heaven," when He said He would take the responsibility to get you there.

Your *joy* in the Christian life will come as you live in

obedience to God's Word. You will be happy as you do what God told you to do. John 15:10, 11 says, "If ye keep my commandments, ye shall abide in my love; even as I have kept my Father's commandments, and abide in his love. These things have I spoken unto you, that my joy might remain in you, and that your joy might be full." Salvation comes through trusting Christ. Assurance comes in believing the written record of Scripture. Joy comes through doing what God told you to do.

You will be a better Christian by making a public decision, putting youself on record that you have accepted Christ as your Saviour and that you intend to follow Him.

Baptism pictures what happened in your heart when you got saved, so it ought to follow salvation. It is a testimony of being raised from death to life; it comes after the decision to trust Christ. It is not a means of getting salvation. Immersion pictures the old nature in you, dead because of sin, doomed to hell, being buried in the ground, and the new creature, born anew, raised up to serve the Lord. Here's the way Romans 6:3-6 explains it: "Know ye not, that so many of us as were baptized into Jesus Christ were baptized into his death? therefore we are buried with him by baptism into death: that like as Christ was raised up from the dead by the glory of the Father, even so we also should walk in newness of life. For if we have been planted together in the likeness of his death, we shall be also in the likeness of his resurrection."

Sixth, share the wonderful news of salvation whenever you can, for "He that winneth souls is wise" (Prov. 11:30). Does one who has dishonored the name of Christ by her actions, does she have a right to tell other people they need to get saved? Oh, yes, yes, yes! You of all people ought to be able to tell of the forgiving grace of God!

Remember the woman of Samaria in the Gospel of

John chapter 4? She had surely "blown it"! She'd been married five times, and she was living with a man with whom she hadn't even gone through the formality of a wedding ceremony. She was the town's notorious adulteress. Jesus tenderly but persistently bored down to the heart of the problem, her sin. After she received forgiveness and salvation, she ran back to the city, calling to the men to "Come, see a man, which told me all things that ever I did: is not this the Christ?" (John 4:29). Then, says verse 39, "Many of the Samaritans of that city believed on him for the saying of the woman, which testified, He told me all that ever I did." This soiled woman, an outcast, was able to lead many of the men in the town to Jesus, because she told them how she'd been forgiven.

So you've blown it; you've spoiled the testimony of other Christians; you've besmirched the name of Jesus. Now give the world a humble and wonderful testimony to God's forgiving grace!

The more earnestly you work at soul winning, the less likely you will be to fall into sin. You will be more conscious and aware of the Holy Spirit's power and less likely to countenance unconfessed sin in your own life.

Surely the forgiven child of God ought to share her wonderful good fortune with others. There are other broken hearts needing the healing touch of the Saviour's hand. There are others who are sickened by their sin, helpless to change themselves. You need to give them the blessed Gospel. Not only will you save them from the agony of a wasted life and eventual hell, but you will find quick forgiveness for your own sins. James 5:20 says, "Let him know, that he which converteth the sinner from the error of his way shall save a soul from death, and shall hide a multitude of sins."

The joyful Christian life is not simply abstention from

sin. It is a gladsome, productive walk with God, growing each day to be more and more like His Son Jesus. What a day it will be when you come "Unto him that is able to keep you from falling, and to present you faultless before the presence of his glory with exceeding joy" (Jude 24).

That is when the reality of the promise God makes in Joel 2:25, 26 will become obvious even to our tear-dimmed eyes. "I will restore to you the years that the locust hath eaten. . . . And ye shall eat in plenty, and be satisfied, and praise the name of the Lord your God, that hath dealt wonderously with you: and my people shall never be ashamed."

This great God, our God, has promised that He not only will blot out the failure and sins of lost years, but that He will give us the blessing and reward, if we turn back to Him now, as if we had been faithful our whole lives through.

chapter seven

'Ways to avoid
Satan's booby traps

"Be sober, be vigilant; because your adversary the devil, as a roaring lion, walketh about, seeking whom he may devour: Whom resist stedfast in the faith"
I Pet. 5:8, 9

"There hath no temptation taken you but such as is common to man: but God is faithful, who will not suffer you to be tempted above that ye are able; but will with the temptation also make a way to escape, that ye may be able to bear it."
I Cor. 10:13

You've taken a deep breath of hope. You have set behind you the heartaches of the past. You have admitted your failures. Now you are setting out to walk the joyful, holy, productive Christian life.

We have to honestly admit that the pathway in the Christian life may be filled with hidden and deadly snares just as a battlefield is often strewn with savage, maiming booby traps.

The Apostle Peter said, "Dearly beloved, I beseech you as strangers and pilgrims, abstain from fleshly lusts, which war against the soul" (I Pet. 2:11). Certain thought patterns and habits make it hard to be a good Christian. Fleshly lusts will war against the soul. "We have met the enemy, and they are us," said Pogo the Possum, the comic strip character. Our own desires can fight our own soul's eternal welfare!

The door bell rang early one Saturday morning at our house. There stood a young woman whose husband had been saved the night before. We'd gone to their home for supper, and after a long and earnest conversation, her husband had knelt to receive Christ as his Saviour. Virginia was so very glad, she'd baked fresh bread and brought it by our house.

"Now," she said eagerly over a cup of coffee, "Tell us all the no-nos. We want to do it right. Tell me all the things we can't do if we're going to be good Christians."

They had attended a liberal and worldly church. They had noticed that in our church we dressed differently; our amusements were different; our life styles were not the same. "Please tell me the no-nos," she said, as if there were certain secret taboos in the Christian life, certain mysterious rites that had to be memorized to earn the right to be called Christian.

I thought of the rhyme we children used to chant, skipping along the sidewalk, "Step on a crack, break your mother's back." In Virginia's mind it was as if the Christian life were not predictable; without cause and effect, with no reasonable standards to govern life by, but only arbitrary, superstitious rules somebody devised to be memorized to avoid being kicked out of the club.

Let's admit it sometimes that's the way it seems to unbelievers when they view the differences in the Christian life style.

I was born in Texas. There, it was not uncommon to see church members stand outside a church between Sunday school and church services, grabbing a quick smoke. But those same people would have been shocked if someone suggested a mixed swimming party for the young people.

When I was a teenager, we moved to Illinois. There, church members would have planned a mixed swimming party for the church young people without a second thought, but the pastor probably preached against the movies, and perhaps also the opera, and he might have discouraged wearing jewelry. Not too many years ago, some earnest Christians waited until after midnight on Sunday to catch a train, so they would not cause someone to sin by having to work on the "Sabbath."

If all Christians had the same list of no-nos, it wouldn't seem so confusing to new believers. But there is a wide difference of opinion among good and dedicated Christians about what is "all right." Seeing that there is little agreement on precisely just what is right or wrong some people are inclined to shuck the whole problem, dismiss it as "legalism," and declare that Christian liberty means they can do anything they like to do anytime they want to do it.

We need to understand that there are dangers in setting artificial standards for our conduct. We could make the list of "things I don't do" too important and not pay enough attention to our heart attitudes. This was a temptation to people living in Bible times, just as it is to us. The Pharisees were meticulously careful about unimportant little rituals while they often lived wicked lives. Jesus said to them, "Woe unto you, scribes and Pharisees, hypocrites! for ye pay tithe of mint and anise and cummin (tiny spices) and have omitted the weightier matters of the law, judgment, mercy and faith: these ought ye to have done, and not to leave the other undone.... Ye make clean the outside of the cup and of the platter, but within they are full of extortion and excess. Thou blind Pharisee, cleanse first that which is within the cup and platter, that the outside of them may be clean also" (Matt. 23:23-26).

Any standard of conduct that does not spring from a right heart attitude is worthless. Right behavior on the outside must spring from an earnest desire on the inside. You ought not simply conform to someone else's standard for public approval. You could carefully keep every no-no you ever heard of and still be a wicked and selfish Christian. Even if, for whatever reason, you made yourself conform for a while to someone else's standard, eventually your heart attitude would reveal itself.

It's wrong, too, to set up a rigid set of rules to use in harshly judging those who don't meet our particular set of no-nos. We long for others to understand that we're trying to do right even if we fail. So we ought to be compassionate with those who don't conform to our standards. "With what judgment ye judge, ye shall be judged," says Matthew 7:2. Whatever we expect of others, that standard is what God will use to judge us.

Furthermore, an arbitrary list of do's and don'ts could lull you into a false sense of security. As long as you aren't doing any of those specific bad things, you might feel immune to temptation. Like Little Jack Horner who pulled out a plum and said, "What a good boy am I!" you could be so proud of the thing you *weren't* doing, you might be caught unaware by real and awful temptation. That's why the Lord warned, "Let him that thinketh he standeth take heed lest he fall" (I Cor. 10:12). The answer lies not in simply making up a list of "thou shalt nots."

However, if we want to live a truly godly life, we'd better acknowledge the sad fact that it sure is easy to do wrong and sure hard to do right! There are dangers in making an arbitrary list of "things good Christians don't do." But there *is* great value in establishing principles to use as guides in making day-to-day decisions.

Principle 1: *If God says in His Word it is wrong, it is wrong.* In the Bible God tells us plainly certain things are right or wrong. One such list is found in Galatians 5:19-24, listing the fruits of the Holy Spirit and the lusts of the flesh. If the

Word of God says a certain act is sin, then it is sin, without regard to circumstances or cultural standards. We don't need to ask if extramarital sex is all right under certain circumstances. The Bible plainly says it is wrong. "What thing soever I command you, observe to do it: thou shalt not add thereto, nor diminish from it" (Deut. 12:32). Cultural standards change. God's standard of morality never changes. Our frail human hearts dart about, looking for excuses why a certain sin might not be really wrong. We must come to the place where we say simply, "When God says it is wrong, it is wrong, and I will not do it."

Principle 2: *Every overt sin had its beginning in the heart.* Sometimes I have felt a temptation to sin strike me like a bolt out of the blue. I wasn't intending to do wrong; temptation just suddenly surged up and overwhelmed me. But rueful honesty compelled me to admit I had "set myself up for it." Perhaps I had been feeling sorry for myself, or had been focusing too much on fleshly things, had permitted myself to covet or envy. Romans 13:14 says, "But put ye on the Lord Jesus Christ, and make not provision for the flesh, to fulfill the lusts thereof." Don't make it easy for yourself to do wrong!

King Solomon warned, "Keep thy heart with all diligence, for out of it are the issues of life" (Prov. 4:23).

It is frightening to see how the human heart can accustom itself to sin. An act that once would have seemed hideous and repulsive can, by contemplating it too often, eventually become attractive.

> *Vice is a monster of so frightful mien,*
> *As to be hated needs but to be seen*

69

> *Yet seen too oft, familiar with her face,*
> *We first endure, then pity, then embrace.*
> Alexander Pope

Many a woman who considered herself to be a "good" Christian, but who permitted her mind to dwell on illicit fantasies, eventually has yielded to flagrant sin. Her conscience became defiled so that sin no longer seemed very sinful to her.

Principle 3: *It is easier to keep the heart and mind clean than it is to cleanse them after they are defiled.* Good housekeepers know it is better to keep the kitchen stove scrubbed regularly than to allow food spills to burn on it and then try to scrub it clean. Proverbs 22:3 says, "A prudent man foreseeth the evil, and hideth himself: but the simple pass on, and are punished." Proverbs 6:27, 28 asks the obvious question, "Can a man take fire in his bosom, and his clothes not be burned? Can one go upon hot coals, and his feet not be burned?"

It might be possible to watch a salacious movie, and then by prayer and self-discipline to erase the images from the soiled mind. But when the mind has been defiled, it is hard to *want* it cleansed. The imprint of sin can leave a lasting scum.

Lot, the nephew of Abraham, chose to move to Sodom, an exceedingly wicked city. Lot was "vexed with the filthy conversation of the wicked." He was a righteous man, II Peter 2:8 tells us, but "in seeing and hearing, vexed his righteous soul from day to day with their unlawful deeds." He chose to associate with ungodly men. He was a righteous man, but his continual contact with evil men eventaully destroyed him, and the last we hear of him in Scripture is his getting drunk in a dark cave and committing incest with his two daughters (Gen. 19:30-38).

So a Christian woman might choose to watch a suggestive television program or read a titillating book. She would still go to Heaven (that was determined when she asked Christ to save her from her sins). But her conscience is going to be defiled, and her concern for spiritual things will be blunted. It will be hard to focus on spiritual things again. Ephesians 4:30 warns us to "grieve not the holy Spirit of God, whereby ye are sealed unto the day of redemption." The blessed Holy Spirit seals us, keeps us, and takes us to Heaven. But He can be grieved and our awareness of His near presence obscured when we contaminate our lives with filth.

Principle 4: *It is impossible to satisfy a fleshly appetite by indulging it.* A tobacco company advertises its products with the claim, "They satisfy." But obviously, they *don't* satisfy. If smokers were truly satisfied when they smoked that brand of cigarette, they'd have no more need to buy more! You cannot make a fleshly lust diminish by feeding it. Ecclesiastes 5:10 says, "He that loveth silver shall not be satisfied with silver; nor he that loveth abundance with increase."

Alcoholics, chain smokers, drug addicts, fat people, and promiscuous people are all sad evidence that to indulge a fleshly lust only reinforces it and makes it stronger, not weaker. The only sure way to control fleshly temptation is to starve it, never to feed it, never to give in to it.

The needs for food, for drink, for sexual satisfaction, and for warmth are all legitimate, God-given needs. But we need to be aware that Satan seeks to twist legitimate needs and desires into lusts that can destroy us.

Principle 5: *If you are tolerant of one sin in your life, you will be vulnerable to other temptations.* My Uncle Bill Rice was a rancher. When we rode the trail together, he often said, "Be sure to close the gate. If you leave just one gate open, every horse in the pasture gets out." "No man can serve two masters," Jesus said in Matthew 6:24, "for either he will hate the one and love the other; or else he will hold to the one, despise the other. Ye cannot serve God and mammon." "Know ye not," asked the Apostle Paul in Romans 6:16, "that to whom ye yield yourselves servants to obey, his servants ye are?"

So a woman who considers herself a moral, good person, but who permits herself an occasional dishonesty may soon find herself enmeshed in other kinds of immorality as well. "He that is faithful in that which is least is faithful also in much: and he that is unjust in the least is unjust also in much" (Luke 16:10).

In I Peter 5:8, it says that our adversary, the devil, is like a roaring lion, seeking whom he may devour. If we permit the enemy access to our lives in only one area, we have nevertheless admitted him into the fortress of our hearts, inside the defenses, where he can work insidiously—and he will! So it is wise to set boundaries for the life, "parameters," standards for conduct, long before the temptation ever comes, so you can say no emphatically when it does arrive.

We ought not to make sin seem ordinary and innocuous by casual conversation. Ephesians 5:3, 4 says, "But fornication, and all uncleaness, or covetousness, let it not be once named among you, as becometh saints; Neither filthiness, nor foolish talking, nor jesting, which are not convenient: but rather giving of thanks." Then verses 11 and 12 say, "And have no fellowship with the unfruitful works of darkness, but rather reprove them. For it is a shame even to speak of those things which are done of them in secret."

Ann was having great marital difficulties. Finally she said to her husband bitterly, "I guess it's no use. We'd just better get a divorce." Later, she told me, "that word *divorce* just hung in the air. I didn't mean to say it, but once I said it out loud, it just hung there between us, and then things went downhill all the way." Now they are divorced. Her three sons have no father. By talking about divorce, she made it seem to be a legitimate option.

Principle 6: *Those who do not love the Lord may not help you to be a good Christian.* "If the world hate you," Jesus said in John 15:18-20, "ye know that it hated me before it hated you. If ye were of the world, the world would love his own: but because ye are not of the world, but I have chosen you out of the world, therefore the world hateth you. Remember the word that I have said unto you, The servant is not greater than his lord. If they have persecuted me, they will also persecute you; if they have kept my saying, they will keep your's also."

You'd think that your unsaved or worldly friends would want you to succeed spiritually, especially if you've made a mess of your life and are trying to put things back together. You may feel betrayed when you discover your "friends" are trying to lure you back to the old ways of sin. But "this world is no friend to grace, to lead us on to Heaven."

The woman living in rebellion against God wants corroboration that the Christian life doesn't work. She wants to believe that good Christians are fakes, hypocrites, not really enjoying living for Christ, so she won't feel guilty. She wants an excuse for not doing right. She will be delighted to see you fall again and may even set you up for the fall! "Lay not wait, O wicked man, against the dwelling of the righteous; spoil not his resting place" (Pro. 24:15). So evil men will try to make you do wrong. They will actively attempt to seduce you to sin. Jesus said to the Pharisees, "Ye compass sea and land to make one proselyte, and when he is made, ye make him twofold more the child of hell than yourselves!"

So resisting temptation means finding friends who love the Lord and associating with them. Spend time with Christians who want you to succeed in your Christian life. Find wise people and listen to them.

This does not mean you must cut yourself off from every contact with those you knew before you started serving God. They may have hearts hungry and eager for a sweet testimony of God's forgiving grace. They may need your encouragement to trust Christ, too. But your intimate friendships ought never to be with those who have no time for Christ. They will actively discourage your trying to live for God.

Principle 7: *The habit you feel does not hurt you may destroy someone who follows you.* It may be true that you can do some things others consider sin, and that it would have no adverse effect on you. But a Christian needs to remember that others following your example can be hurt by a temptation that doesn't touch you.

Medical statistics indicate that of nine people who ever drink intoxicating liquor, one will have a drinking problem. Of every thirteen people who ever drink, one will become an alcoholic. *You* may be able to "handle your liquor," although the truth is, all drunkards once thought they could "handle their liquor" too. But who is it you might doom to a lifetime of misery and regret because they followed your example?

My husband and I have seven children. Three of them are now married. One son has a baby boy. That makes thirteen in our immediate family. If I served liquor to my family only occasionally, statistics predict that I would doom one of those precious lives to a lifetime of tragic alcoholism!

A woman might enjoy ballroom dancing with her own husband. Her daughter, following her mother's example and dancing with a boyfriend, might find the sexual excitement and arousal of the dance more temptation than she can handle, and she could lose her purity. That's a high price to pay for the freedom of doing what you want to do! Romans 14:7 says, "For none of us liveth to himself, and no man dieth to himself."

The choices we make about our amusements and life style might be easy if no one else were affected by our choices. But others are affected by what we do. They see; they imitate; they use our lives as a pattern for theirs, perhaps to their lasting harm.

"All things are lawful for me," Paul said, "but all things are not expedient." It would not be morally wrong for him to do certain things, Paul was saying; nevertheless, they might not really help him spiritually. "All things are lawful for me, but all things edify not. Let no man seek his own, but every man another's wealth" (I Cor. 10:23, 24).

In I Corinthians 8:8-13, the Apostle Paul said, "Meat commendeth us not to God: for neither, if we eat, are we the better; neither, if we eat not, are we the worse. But take heed lest by any means this liberty of your's become a stumblingblock to them that are weak. For if any man see thee which hast knowledge sit at meat in the idol's temple, shall not the conscience of him which is weak be emboldened to eat those things which are offered to idols? And through thy knowledge shall the weak brother perish, for whom Christ died? But when ye sin so against the brethren, and wound their weak conscience, ye sin against Christ. Wherefore, if meat make my brother to offend, I will eat no flesh while the world standeth, lest I make my brother to offend."

Surely there are enough exciting and happy things to do in God's great creation for relaxation and amusement, that we don't need to choose those that would hurt others! It may take some imaginative and diligent planning, but there is a tremendous variety of entertainment and activities available to the child of God that would strengthen and refresh rather than defile.

Principle 8: *It is impossible to fight a fleshly temptation with fleshly weapons.* Sometimes I've been so heartsick about my sin, I've wished I could physically pound on the old devil for tempting me! But that won't work. He's much too strong for me. If I am to gain the victory over temptation I must do it God's way. In II Corinthians 10:3-5 it says, "For though we walk in the flesh, we do not war after the flesh: (For the weapons of our warfare are not carnal, but mighty through God to the pulling down of strong holds.) Casting down imaginations, and every high thing that exalteth itself against the knowledge of God, and bringing into captivity every thought to the obedience of Christ." The clue here is "mighty *through God.*" I must take all these things that assault my mind and bring them to Jesus. "Here they are, Jesus, all those dirty, wicked things that tempt me—I'm capturing them and bringing them to submit them to You."

We once had a steer named Rochester, who loved to jump the fences and leave our farm. One day a farmer called to say

Rochester was eating his corn and would we please come to get him. My husband put on his cowboy boots and hat, grabbed a rope, and drove over to the Smiths' farm.

"Where's that ornery critter?" he asked Mrs. Smith.

She misunderstood him. "He's on the couch reading the newspaper," she answered. When they got the various "hims" sorted out, my husband went to the barn to get Rochester and bring him home. But Rochester didn't want to come. He liked Mr. Smith's corn! My husband and son John heaved and pushed and threatened and whacked, all to no avail. Finally, my husband tied a rope around Rochester's horns, tied the other end to the bumper of the car, and hauled Rochester home. Rochester skidded down the highway, spraddle-legged, hooves scraping, balking and fighting every inch of the way, but home he came. (And he ended up in the family freezer, too, which taught us all a hard lesson concerning stubbornness!)

That is what you must do with the thoughts and imaginations that vaunt themselves against God. Capture them, drag them under the control of the Saviour, and expect the Lord Jesus to give you the help you need in controlling them. "Greater is he that is in you, than he that is in the world," says I John 4:40. You cannot win this battle with your flesh. You must have the power of God; it is a *spiritual* warfare.

My friend Becky had a chronic, long standing weight problem. She'd gone on all the crash diets and programs and tried all the pills and exercises. Nothing had worked. One day she said, "Lord, you promised you'd help me. I'm weak. I can't help myself. Please give me the grace to do right." She lost sixty-seven pounds and has never regained them. She has since become a wonderful help in encouraging other women who need to lose weight. It was spiritual warfare, won in the power of the Holy Spirit, not by the flesh.

77

Principle 9: *The freedom to choose ends when you have made your choice; the consequences of your choices are inevitable and incalculable.* A woman may sense the beginnings of her sin; there is no way she can guess at the awful outreachings of it. "Know ye not, that to whom ye yield yourselves servants to obey, his servants ye are to whom ye obey; whether of sin unto death, or of obedience unto righteousness?" (Rom. 6:16).

If you choose forgiveness and restoration in Christ, then you become the Lord's bondservant. But serving Him won't seem like bondage at all, because He loves you and wants you to be eternally happy.

But if you choose your own way, the way of sin, then you become the servant of sin, and the bondage is terrible in its consequences.

Witness the pitiful victims of the cigarette habit. Often smokers who have had a laryngectomy for cancer of the throat caused by cigarette smoking continue to smoke cigarettes by holding them to the breathing holes cut in their throats! How long, how tedious, how burdensome are the unavoidable chains of sin! Proverbs 5:22, 23 says, "His own iniquities shall take the wicked himself, and he shall be holden with the cords of his sins. He shall die without instruction; and in the greatness of his folly he shall go astray."

Suppose you do have to say "no" to an activity you have realized hurts you spiritually. There's no need to put on a doleful expression and whine, "I wish I could do that, but I'm a Christian now, so I can't!"—with the implication that being a good Christian sure is a rocky, unhappy, boring way to live!

Instead, why not thank God with all your heart that

you don't need to enjoy the fleeting pleasures of sin in order to have true joy? Moses knew that sin's pleasure is very temporary, so he chose "rather to suffer affliction with the people of God than to enjoy the pleasures of sin for a season; Esteeming the reproach of Christ greater riches than the treasures in Egypt; for he had respect unto the recompence of the reward" (Heb. 11:25, 26).

King Solomon said the "bread of deceit is sweet to man; but afterwards his mouth shall be filled with gravel" (Prov. 20:17). Proverbs 9:17, 18 says that "Stolen waters are sweet, and bread eaten in secret is pleasant. But he knoweth not that the dead are there, and that her guests are in the depths of hell."

Sin is fun—for a little while. But the chains of habit will bind, and the bitter, grinding results will last and last. Don't ever feel sorry for yourself because you have chosen to do right. That's the path of the just, like a shining light, that shineth more and more unto the perfect day" (Prov. 4:18). As for the wicked, the next verse says, "The way of the wicked is as darkness. They know not what they stumble at."

Principle 10: *Once a life has been defiled by a sin, that sin may never again seem quite as terrible as it really is.* It may be that the human spirit could not survive if we understood how sinful our sin really is. If we can't cope with the magnitude of our wickedness, we might decide it isn't so terrible after all.

Suppose a woman has been unfaithful to her husband and committed adultery with another man. She has climbed over a God erected barrier that she may never be able to rebuild quite as strong as it was. Unless she guards her mind and heart with particular care when temptation comes again, she may more easily succumb, just because she has lost her horror of sin's wickedness.

King Hezekiah sensed this. God had sent the prophet Isaiah to him to tell him to put his house in order because he was going to die. With earnest tears, Hezekiah asked the Lord to spare his life. God granted his request. Instead of being humble and grateful to God for His special grace, Hezekiah reacted with arrogance and pride. "In those days Hezekiah was sick to the death, and prayed unto the Lord: and he spake unto him and he gave him a sign. But Hezekiah rendered not again according to the benefit done unto him; for his heart was lifted up: therefore there was wrath upon him, and upon Judah and Jerusalem. Notwithstanding Hezekiah humbled himself for the pride of his heart, both he and the inhabitants of Jerusalem, so that the wrath of the Lord came not upon them in the days of Hezekiah" (II Chron. 32:24-26).

In answer to God's forgiveness, King Hezekiah said, "What shall I say: he hath both spoken unto me and himself done it: I shall go softly all my years in the bitterness of my soul" (Isa. 38:15).

So ought we to walk softly and carefully once we have sinned, recognizing how fragile is the barrier we have built against sin and how easily it can be breached again.

These are ten important principles by which you can measure your choices. How important it is not simply to conform to someone else's standards of conduct, but to make thoughtful and careful choices, compassionate of the needs of others and aware of your own weaknesses.

chapter eight

**Rebuilding
damaged
relationships**

"Humble yourselves therefore under the mighty hand of God, that he may exalt you in due time: Casting all your care upon him; for he careth for you."

I Pet. 5:6,7

If starting all over again involved only our relationship with God, accepting His forgiveness, and the setting out to do right day by day, the task would be fairly simple, if not always easy!

But it isn't simple or easy. Those you love have been hurt and wronged by your behavior. There is no magic ink eradicator that will blot out their memories of heartsick disappointment in you. You have changed, you say. You've admitted your sin. You've set out to build the right kind of habits. But they only sigh and say, "I've heard that song before."

It is said that people tend to trust absolute strangers more than they trust their own family and friends. Why? Because the stranger has not disappointed them yet. When you set out to rebuild a damaged relationship, you don't start out at zero on the scale of trust. You start out at minus thirty or maybe even minus fifty!

It isn't that you are traveling the same road simply at

a different speed or even that you are stalled on the same road. Instead, you have been recklessly rushing in the opposite direction down the road of mutual trust. So you have an enormous amount of ground to make up. And at some point along the way back, you are going to be tempted to say, "It isn't worth the struggle."

However, for the sake of the ones you've wronged in the past, you *must* make yourself do right day after day, week after week, even year after year, without regard to the responses of other people. Do right simply because it is right, not because you want to manipulate someone into doing what you want them to do.

Be willing to have your past thrown up to you. God forgives and forgets. Often people don't. They may not be deliberately vindictive. They may simply be heartsick of the problem. "Hope deferred maketh the heart sick," Proverbs 13:12 says. The one you love may be only trying to guard his heart from being sick with disappointment again. So don't expect your declaration of intent to do right to be met with hurrahs of joy. It may, instead, be met with the silence of skepticism!

Micah 7:9 says, "I will bear the indignation of the Lord, because I have sinned against him, until he plead my cause, and execute judgment for me: he will bring me forth to the light, and I shall behold his righteousness." In Micah 7:7, 8 Micah expresses the faith by which he intends to act until God does intervene in his behalf: "Therefore I will look unto the Lord; I will wait for the God of my salvation: my God will hear me. Rejoice not against me, O mine enemy: when I fall, I shall arise; when I sit in darkness, the Lord shall be a light unto me."

I Peter 5:6 makes the promise, "Humble yourselves therefore under the mighty hand of God that he may exalt you in due time." If you humble yourself, then God will, at the proper time (perhaps not as soon as you would wish), raise you up. Meanwhile, God says in verse 7, you are to cast "all your care upon him; for he careth for you." God will be with you while you wait for others to learn to love you and respect you.

Don't expect others to take their share of the blame for what happened. Now that God has given you a heart to want to do right, you may long for those you love and are accountable for to serve God with you. Let the Lord deal with them with the same gentleness and mercy He exercised so tenderly with you.

Remember, you can do the will of God today, where you find yourself, with the commitments you have already made.

Did you marry out of the will of God, perhaps someone who is not a child of God? Nevertheless, it is God's will for you to stay married to that one. Jesus said in Matthew 19:6, "What therefore God hath joined together, let not man put asunder." This He said in answer to a question about the legitimacy of divorce—where two people might think they had married in error and so seek a divorce. Even those two, Jesus said, have been joined by God; the marriage is not to be dissolved. So one aspect of God's will for your life now includes your staying married to the one you married and promised to love until death parted you, however ignorantly or rebelliously you made the choice.

Perhaps you once thought God called you to be a missionary. Then you lost sight of that goal, married, and had a family. It may be that now you cannot travel as a missionary because of home responsibilities. But there are people living near you who desperately need the Lord Jesus. It is eternally important for them to hear the Gospel through you now. Today you can win them to Jesus.

It might be you wasted the opportunity to go to college,

and now you daily regret the lack of training. But there are things you can learn now, outside a formal classroom. There is some way you can meet your daily responsibilities and still learn what you need to learn in order to serve God well.

Did you neglect your children and waste the precious years of their childhood? You cannot turn back the clock. But you can, today, be the kind of mother a grown daughter or son needs. Children never get too old to need a wise and loving mother!

It may be that because of wrong choices made in the past, you have destroyed any opportunity to serve God in the place you once held. Some relationships or some ministries might be forever closed to you. "If the tree fall toward the south or toward the north, in the place where the tree falleth, there shall it be" (Eccl. 11:3). A preacher's wife, having run off with another man and then coming to see how wrong she'd been, might not be able to resume the duties of a pastor's wife. But she could find something to do for God: cleaning the church, cooking Saturday morning breakfast for the bus workers, or making visual aids for a busy Sunday school teacher. She might forfeit the right to leadership but she can still do *something* God needs done.

Rebuild where you can. You may have forfeited the opportunity to guide your own children to maturity. That doesn't cut you off from helping someone else's child in need. If you stole money from an employer, you may never be made comptroller of a company. But there are literally hundreds of jobs you could do well and prove yourself in, without ever having to handle cash again. You can do the will of God today in the place where you find yourself.

Sanctify the scars left by the healing of the wound. I once counseled with a young woman named Carolyn, who had betrayed her husband and daughter by going to live with another man. After several years of living in sin, she came to realize what a wicked life it was. Now, what in the world was she to do?

I showed her Psalm 130:3, 4: "If thou, Lord, shouldest mark iniquities, O Lord, who shall stand? But there is forgiveness with thee, that thou mayest be feared."

"But you don't understand!" she sobbed. "I've spoiled everything. It's like I'd torn a gaping hole here in my skirt. It's there. It can't ever be mended. I've ruined everything!"

"No, no, Carolyn. It's not like a torn skirt. Let me tell you what it's like. Last month the doctor told me a test I'd taken indicated that I had breast cancer. I went to the hospital to have surgery. As a result of that surgery, I now have an ugly, swollen, red gash across my breast. But let me tell you what I feel when I look at that disfiguring scar. I feel not regret, not shame, oh, no, but rather a deep, overwhelming sense of gratitude to God that that horrible cancer cell could be cut out and destroyed!"

That's how a child of God must feel about the scars left by the excising of sin from the life. Thank God there is a remedy! Thank God that though you are a sinner, you are a forgiven sinner. Fornicators, idolaters, adulterers, effeminate, homosexuals, thieves, covetous, drunkards, revilers, and extortioners cannot enter Heaven, I Corinthians 6:9, 10 says. "And such were some of you," says verse 11, "but ye are washed, but ye are sanctified, but ye are justified in the name of the Lord Jesus and by the Spirit of our God." You are no longer a sinner. As we said in chapter three, you will cope for the rest of your life with the reality of sin in your everyday experience. God, your heavenly father, concerned with your welfare, will discipline His child. But God, acting as your judge, pronounces you no longer a sinner, because the debt for your sin is paid. He counts you righteous because you are wrapped in the robes of Jesus' righteousness (Isa. 61:10). You are washed, and sanctified, and justified! Sanctify the scars that remain! Let them be a constant reminder of your vulnerability to sin and the loving forgiveness of a holy God.

"This one thing I do, forgetting those things which are behind, and reaching forth unto those things which are before, I press toward the mark for the prize of the high calling of God in Christ Jesus" (Phil. 3:13, 14).

Suppose you are the wronged party. What if the one you love has wronged you, and he is trying to start all over again to rebuild the relationship? Let me encourage you to take whatever steps you need to make it easy for him to do right.

Has your home been destroyed by a man who spent money wildly? It wouldn't be surprising if you feel mistreated when you must do without and economize. The problem was none of your making. Why do *you* have to suffer? I beg you to ask the Lord to help you gladly make whatever sacrifices are needed to get the family finances back in order. You can afford to pinch pennies, to make sacrifices, to do without things you really deserve in order to help a man come back to a place of usefulness to God.

Are you married to an alcoholic who has repented of his sin and now trying to do right? Don't say sarcastically, "I wonder how long you'll last this time." Don't begrudge giving up alcoholic beverages yourself. Don't insist on going to places where liquor is served, where the horrible craving for liquor can be aroused again.

If your husband went into sin because of the kinds of friends he had, then gladly give up that circle of friends who will try to draw him back into the old ways. Encourage him to make friends with born-again Christians. Don't hang onto old sins, old ways, old habits yourself, when they will make it difficult for your husband to do right.

Do you have a child who lived in rebellion, who now comes with tears to confess his or her rebellion, promising to do right? Make it easy for the prodigal to do right! Decide the really important things that you must insist he or she do right; and ease up on the less important problems. "Thy gentleness hath made me great," David said in II Samuel 22:36. Be gentle! Children can get easily discouraged, as Colossians 3:21 says. Don't sit back with arms folded, with the attitude, "O. K., Buddy, prove it. Let's see if you really meant what you said." Rather, tenderly, gently lead your child along the right way.

"If thou, Lord, shouldest mark iniquities, O Lord, who shall stand? But there is forgiveness with thee," says Psalm 130:3, 4, "that thou mayest be feared." Loving compassion, full forgiveness, gentleness, all will encourage the one who has sinned to try to do right.

"Whoso causeth the righteous to go astray in an evil way, he shall fall himself into his own pit" (Prov. 28:10). Make it easy for the penitent heart to begin again!

chapter nine

Restoring a broken marriage

"But now in Christ Jesus ye who sometimes were far off are made nigh by the blood of Christ. For he is our peace, who hath made both one, and hath broken down the middle wall of partition between us."
Eph. 2:13, 14

Perhaps the most difficult of all human relationships to restore is a marriage, especially one broken by unfaithfulness. If you are the one who wronged your mate, let me suggest several things for you to keep in mind.

First, you need to ask the Lord to help you realize the enormity of your sin. In the act of marriage, God makes of two different people one flesh. Your marriage was established by God, sanctified by the most holy kind of covenant a human being can make. When a married person defiles that relationship by turning to a third person, he or she shreds and mutilates living quivering flesh.

It may be that your marriage partner is so devastated that he feels it is impossible to restore the marriage. The answer is not for you to become indignant. Remember, *you* were the cause of the problem. So you'll have to prove, perhaps with long patience, that you are trustworthy.

Because you have robbed your mate of something that was his right, you must understand he will continually be

coping with suddenly remembered hurts and fighting suf-
focating emotions for a long time.

I remember one man who for years had felt unease
about his wife's faithfulness. Time and time again she had
professed her love and chided him for his doubts. For years
he carried a load of guilt, not understanding why he didn't
trust his wife. You can see why his resentment was intense,
when it eventually came out that she really *had* been unfaithful to him through those years. It was difficult for
him to forget the years of shame he'd lived feeling himself
an unworthy Christian because he couldn't erase his doubts
about his wife. When his wife repented and wanted to start
over, he wanted to forgive her. But he had to deal with every
memory of those long years, one by one, as they came to
haunt him. No wonder it took a long time for him to fully
forgive his wife and finally forget the bitter past!

When you make your confession of sin, be sure to
handle the whole scope of your unfaithfulness, not just the
particulars in which you have been found out. No matter
what your intentions might be in not confessing it all, the
impact on your mate will be doubly hurtful if new evidence
of unfaithfulness comes to light. That's like cutting off the
puppy's tail a little at a time!

So take your losses at the very beginning. Confess
everything. Don't be trapped by confessing only what is
already known. That's what Achan did, as told in Joshua
7:20, 21. He confessed very freely his sin—*after* he had been
caught! Determine that you'll leave nothing hidden in your
heart, either to tempt you further or to grieve your marriage
partner when it does come to light.

However, I strongly advise that you not give the intimate details of the affair, not what days, nor where, nor how
often, no matter how tearfully your spouse insists on the

details. That only lends fire to the imagination and makes the past too vivid to forget.

Sometimes a sinning partner finds the load of guilt so heavy he confesses all the sordid details and then feels a great relief from the burden. But that often only places the burden on the wronged partner, rather than erasing it. Ask the Lord to help you know how to handle the confession so that it is complete and honest, but discreet in the exposure of details.

It might be necessary for a wife to tell her husband that she finds their friendship with a certain couple to be tempting. She ought to be discreet in sharing her need for protection, but still convey to her husband that intimate friendship with that particular couple leaves her vulnerable to temptation.

Expect there to be a time of grief and mourning. Just as there would be with any other kind of great tragedy in your family—a loss of a home by fire, the death of a child, a financial disaster—so there must be a time to learn to be reconciled to the loss.

You must understand that though you would like forgiveness and forgetting and it never to be mentioned again, this is nearly impossible. Questions will come up, and they must be answered patiently, without anger, acknowledging again that it was your act that caused the grief. Be willing to express, again and again your love and affection, your sorrow for the grief you caused, and your dedication to making things right.

When questions do arise, don't ever permit comparison of that paramour and your mate. Don't call him by name. Don't ever try to explain what attracted you to him, nor what you found good in him. Nor should you seize that as an opportunity to explain why you fell into sin, that your husband was distracted, unloving, too pious, or unattractive. There might be, at some time in the future, an occasion you could express your emotional needs to your spouse, but never when he is desperately seeking reassurance and healing.

Should you make a public confession and apology? The Bible principle is that you ought to ask forgiveness of those you've wronged (James 5:16; Matt. 18:15-17). If there was a flagrant and open breaking of God's laws and if many in the church were hurt by the scandal, then perhaps a public confession should be made. Often the best way to do this is to go forward at the invitation at the end of the church service, and ask the church's forgiveness for being a reproach without being explicit about the nature of the sin.

Public acknowledgment of public sin, restoration and public rededication are all important. It gives Christian brothers and sisters an opportunity to express their gladness that you are wanting to live for God again and burdens them to pray for you. It takes away the excuses of those who use another's sin for going into sin themselves. Will it be embarrassing and humiliating? It certainly will! But that humiliation will prove to be a tremendous deterrent if you ever were tempted to stray again. "God resisteth the proud," I Peter 5:5 says, "and giveth grace to the humble." God will give you grace to make whatever public confession you ought to make, and He will make it an encouragement to others.

To the wife who was the injured mate I would say, ask the Lord to open your heart to your own needs and failures. Often, in cases of marital infidelity, the innocent mate somehow failed to meet the needs of the wanderer. You may have already done some searching of heart about the matter, and, if you are absolutely honest with yourself, you already know in what areas you failed. It would be right for you to confess these to your mate, and promise to strive to meet his needs more completely. It may be very important for you to dig deeply into your own heart to take responsibility for your share of the blame, so your mate will know that you are also aware of the problems so that you both can fix them. Otherwise, he might have no hope of things working out.

Listen to what *he* says he wants in you. Many a good woman blithely hurtles down the road to failure, thinking she knows exactly what her husband wants and needs; she never seems to hear what he is trying to tell her he *really* wants. Don't you decide what's best for him and then administer it willy-nilly. Let the one who owns your body (as Corinthians 7:4 says) determine how you use it. Listen to him. Find out what he really wants. Then meet those God-given needs.

This is the man you married. He has some elemental character flaws, perhaps, but he had those when you married him. Perhaps you didn't recognize them then, but that was because of flaws in your own character and personality. Nor can you promise him that you will never fail him in any area of life.

So you must forgive him. If you would have God forgive you for your sin, you must forgive the man who wronged you. Jesus taught us to pray, "And forgive us our debts, (our sins) as we forgive our debtors" (Matt. 6:12). Then He continued, "For if ye forgive men their trespasses, your heavenly Father will also forgive you: But if ye forgive not men their trespasses, neither will your Father forgive your trespasses" (Matt. 6:14, 15). Then in Matthew 7:1-4, He said, "Judge not, that ye be not judged. For with what judgment ye judge, ye shall be judged: and with what measure ye mete, it shall be measured to you again. And why beholdest thou the mote that is in thy brother's eye, but considerest not the beam that is in thine own eye? Or how wilt thou say to thy brother Let me pull out the mote out of thine eye; and, behold, a beam is in thine own?"

You may not have sinned the particular sin of adultery, but you have sinned, and you too surely need God's forgiveness. So you must forgive this man who has sinned so grievously. Forgive him even when he doesn't seem to understand how greatly he has injured you. Yes, he has betrayed you. Humanly speaking, that is unforgivable. But you must forgive him, as God, for Christ's sake, forgave you (Eph. 4:32). G. K. Chesterton said, "Forgiveness means forgiving the unforgivable, if it is to have any virtue at all."

Resist the temptation to dig for details. Don't make him relive the sin by stirring up his memory. No matter how hard he wants to do right, if you force him to remember his sin by talking about it, he may be ensnared by it again. The more you talk about it, the more legitimate the relationship will seem to become.

Nor is it wise, it seems to me, for a wife to "have it out" with the other woman. You probably ought not to have any contact with her at all. Don't threaten her. Don't berate her. Leave her alone. You cannot build a fence high enough to keep your husband from wandering. You'll have to bind him to your heart with cords of love, not threats.

Be careful not to use his past sin as a club over his head to keep him in line. I remember a wife who referred regularly to "that terrible thing you did in Chicago." It was not a surprise to see that man lose all heart in trying to please his wife and eventually turn to someone else.

A woman may be tempted to use her husband's former unfaithfulness for an excuse for escapades of her own— spending too much money on clothing, flirting, getting fat, or not cleaning her house. You are accountable to God for your own behavior, regardless of the circumstances. Don't "pay back" a man for the hurts he has caused you.

I would earnestly beg the woman reading this who is contemplating breaking up her marriage because of a husband's infidelity, to reconsider. In Matthew 19:5, 6 the Lord Jesus said that God created man and woman to be one flesh in marriage. A man was to leave his father and mother and to cleave to his wife. Since it was God who joined them together, no man has a right to put asunder that one flesh. It's significant to notice that God said that *He* joined the two, making them one, about every marriage, not just those we think of as "made in Heaven." The marriage act is the commitment to a lifetime of fidelity and care for the partner, regardless of the circumstances of the marriage, the fitness of the marriage, or even the emotions of the husband and wife.

The Pharisees, asking these questions not to learn, but to "tempt" Jesus asked, "Then why did Moses command to give a writing of divorcement, and to put her away?" They were referring to Deuteronomy 24:1-4. There God gives instructions that if a man married a woman and "hath found some uncleanness in her: then let him write her a bill of divorcement, and give it in her hand, and send her out of his house. And when she is departed out of his house, she may go and be another man's wife." The word *uncleaness* used in this passage is the Hebrew word *ervah*, "a thing offensive." Elsewhere in Scripture it is translated as *nakedness*, referring to sexual sin, as in Ezekiel 23:29. So this Scripture seems to indicate (and Jesus interpreted it so) that marriage could be broken by adultery, but only by adultery.

The Pharisees asked another question. Why did God, in the Law of Moses, make such a provision for divorce, if, as Jesus insisted, God makes a man and his wife one flesh? Jesus' answer was unequivocal: God made the provision for divorce because man is a sinner, "for the hardness of your hearts." God's standard for marriage is that two become one keep their marriage vow to "love him, comfort him, honor, obey, and keep him, in sickness and in health; and forsaking all others, keep thee only unto him so long as ye both shall live."

Men and women often break their marriage vows. They may not cleave to the one they promised to cleave to. Some will not keep the holy vows they made before a holy God. Since some may reject God's way and be unfaithful in marriage, God made provision for the spouse who cannot make the marriage partner do right.

The release by divorce from a marriage is given for one reason only: fornication, or continual adultery. Divorce is permitted because a third party shreds apart the one flesh of the marriage, forcing an alien body between. "What? know ye not that he which is joined to an harlot is one body . . . Flee fornication. Every sin that a man doeth is without the body; but he that committeth fornication sinneth against his own body" (I Cor. 6:16-18).

But the Lord Jesus certainly does not *require* a divorce in the case of adultery. He permitted it so that a woman (or a man), continually sinned against, blatantly sinned against, could be released from the humiliation and rejection not of his or her making and not within his or her power to save.

Not only does the Lord not require a woman to get a divorce, He encourages her to keep the marriage intact, if at all possible, so that her husband may come to know the Lord as his Saviour, too. "The woman which hath an husband that believeth not, and if he be pleased to dwell with her, *let her not leave him.* For the unbelieving husband is sanctified by the wife, and the unbelieving wife is sanctified by the husband: else were your children unclean; but now are they holy. But if the unbelieving depart, let him depart. A brother or a sister is not under bondage in such cases: but God hath called us to peace" (I Cor. 7:13-15). (Remember, "for the hardness of your hearts" God made the rule. If you have done all that you humanly can to save your marriage, then God does not fault you!) But then comes this sweet reassurance, "For what knowest thou, O wife, whether thou shalt save thy husband? or how knowest thou, O man, whether thou shall save thy wife?" (I Cor. 13:16).

The marriage partner, sinned against but still loving, may well win the sinning mate! This is also the thrust of I Peter 3:1, "Likewise, ye wives, be in subjection to your own husbands; that, if any obey not the word, they may without the word be won by the conversation [behavior—that is not words, but actions] of the wife." An unfaithful, unregenerate husband may be won to Christ by an obedient, Spirit-filled, and patient wife.

This plainly shows that God does not require a woman who has been wronged by an adulterous husband to seek a divorce. On the contrary, He encourages her to try to win him back and save his soul from hell by her meek and quiet spirit. (For detailed handling of this Biblical principle, see my book, *Me? Obey Him?* published by Sword of the Lord Publishers, Murfreesboro, Tennessee, 37130.)

There are strong and urgent reasons for keeping the home intact if at all possible. The children will prosper more physically, financially, spiritually, and emotionally, if they can see their own father rebuild after failure. They will learn not to give up when they have done wrong. They will not have to go through the trauma of having to choose between the two poeple in the world they love most and want to be with. They will learn the sanctity of marriage and the importance of commitment to their own marriages, at whatever the cost, by seeing your faithfulness. They will have the joy of being reared by their own father, not a substitute father or no father at all.

Surely the husband, forgiven and given a chance to restore a broken marriage, would be eternally blessed by the chance to do it right after he'd "blown it." How many a man turns down the road to despair and a wasted life after a divorce! How sweet it would be to put all his strengths and energies into caring for those he deeply loves and for whom he has been given the lifetime responsibility of nurture and care by God. For the sake of that soul, Christ died to save, glorify, and restore your marriage, if it is at all possible.

For your own sake, you should try to save your marriage. Remember those sweet girlhood dreams and longings for somone to love? Remember those golden days of early love? Remember the good years of marriage you enjoyed before this tragedy? They will all be tarnished with sadness and regret if the marriage is broken. Nor would it be easy for you to enter into marriage with someone else, having learned "men can't be trusted." Nor can you possibly supply all the needs of your children: They need the strength and wisdom and love of their own father. How much better it would be to ask God to give you a forgiving, forgetting, and loving heart that by faith in God's ability to help, accepts again the man God gave you to love and cherish!

It's true—I don't know how badly you've been hurt. But Jesus does. The admonition in I Peter 3:1 for a wife's obedience to her husband says it is to be like Christ's obedience ("likewise"). I Peter 2:21-24 describes how Christ responded when He was reviled and threatened. "When he suffered, he threatened not; but committed himself to him that judgeth righteously." He was mistreated; He was maligned; He was abused by God-haters; He was crucified on an infamous cross. But He still prayed, "Father, forgive them; for they know not what they do" (Luke 23:24). If Jesus could forgive them, then you can forgive the one who has wronged you so badly and forget the wrong as Christ said you should. He is your example.

If you will not forgive, I promise you there will come a day when you will say with bitter regret, "I wish I'd tried harder to save my marriage." God can give you the strength and wisdom, the love and compassion you need to make this flawed marriage the precious and holy relationship God had in mind when He brought you together. There is blessed hope, even for the marriage shattered by sin.

chapter ten

Is it ever too late?

"To day if ye will hear his voice, harden not your hearts."
Heb. 4:7

Sarah, the wife of the Bible patriarch Abraham, said it was too late for her. "Look, I couldn't have a baby when I was young and healthy. I certainly can't have a baby now." She was 90 years old, her husband 100. For years she had prayed for a baby, but her arms were empty, and her heart was bitter.

Then God Himself came down and talked with Abraham. "At the time appointed I will return unto thee, ... and Sarah shall have a son," He promised. Sarah conceived and bore a son, when she named Isaac, "Laughter." She said that all the world would laugh with her, the woman who thought it was too late to bear a son.

Martha, the sister of Lazarus, said it was too late for her too. "Lord, if you'd come four days ago, then my brother wouldn't have died. Now it's too late." But it is never too late when Jesus confronts you with your need. Martha saw her dead brother come out of the grave, alive, and she embraced him joyfully (John 11:44).

Bathsheba would have told you she'd really blown it. She was married to Uriah, one of the bravest and most loyal of all King David's soldiers. While Uriah was away, fighting for his king, Bathsheba grew careless. The king happened to see her bathing. He sent for her, committed adultery with her, and sent her home again. When she found she was pregnant, she sent word to him. King David killed her husband and took her as his wife. God in judgment took the life of the little baby she bore. (Thank God He never lets us go on in our sin without dealing with us!) Bathsheba was an adulteress and perhaps an accomplice to murder, but she was penitent, and God was not through with her. He gave her another baby, whom she named Solomon. He became the next great King of Israel (II Sam. 11, 12). Another of Bathsheba's sons, Nathan, established the line through whom the Lord Jesus would come (Luke 3:31).

The preface to this book tells about four women who made wrong choices in their lives. Each of them would have told you that the consequences of their decisions were unchangeable. But that was before they learned about God's wonderful plan to restore them and use them again.

Thelma, who stayed drunk for fifteen years, heard the Gospel and trusted Christ as her Saviour. Though she was a woman of refinement and culture, she humbled herself to admit that she was an "ordinary drunk." She committed herself to a Christian home for alcoholics. While there, she studied the Bible, memorized Scripture, and learned how to cope with temptation, all the time submitting to the stringent rules of the home. When she came back home, she got a job in a department store. In the eight years since she has worked there, she has become such a valuable employee that they have asked her to stay rather than retire.

Eunice, the woman whose affair with another man

ended after the birth of his child, set out to rebuild her relationship with her husband, the man she'd wronged so greatly. The road has been rocky and difficult, and the way often unclear. But now her husband thanks God for the birth of that baby girl, because he found Christ as his Saviour as a result. That was the beginning of a new life for the whole family. They would say that God had given them "beauty for ashes, the oil of joy for mourning, the garment of praise for the spirit of heaviness" (Isa. 61:3).

Phyllis, the woman who stole several thousand dollars from her employer, did confess the theft to him, fully expecting to be sent to jail. Instead, her employer permitted her to pay back all she owed, a week at a time. Now the entire sum has been repaid with interest. You cannot imagine the joy that lights her face and the openness of her relationship with her family, since she confessed her sin and made it right.

And Becky, the woman who wanted to be a missionary but married an unsaved man—can you guess what good thing God did in her life? After several years of patient obedience and earnest prayer, Becky saw her husband trust Christ as his Saviour, surrender to God to be a preacher, and go to Bible school to get ready! For many years now he has pastored a thriving, soul-winning church. Becky's early dream of being a missionary has been fulfilled in the dozens of missionaries her church sends out all over the world. How can I describe the gladness Becky feels when she wakes up to each new day?

It was not too late for these women. Can it be too late for *you*?

No, it is not too late for you, if you will turn to God today. His promises are for today, not tomorrow. The children of Israel were not given forever to repent of their sins and turn back to God. They were limited to a certain time—*today.* "Again, he limiteth a certain day, saying in David, To day, after so long a time; as it is said, To day if ye will hear his voice, harden not your hearts" (Heb. 4:7).

Why does God offer you only today? Because putting off the decision hardens the heart. If you do not do it today, you may not want to do it tomorrow. "Take heed, brethren, lest there be in any of you an evil heart of unbelief, in departing from the living God. But exhort one another daily, while it is called To day; lest any of you be hardened through the deceitfulness of sin" (Heb. 3:12, 13).

How foolish it would be to say, "I'll do it tomorrow"! What advantage would you gain by waiting until tomorrow? Proverbs 29:1 warns, "He, that being often reproved hardeneth his neck, shall suddenly be destroyed, and without remedy." Proverbs 27:1 says, "Boast not thyself of tomorrow; for thou knowest not what a day may bring forth."

Today is the day.

Today is the only day.

Today is the day God wants to begin that good work of restoration in *your* life. Why not let Him?

It won't do to say, "I'll make a bargain with You, God. If You'll promise to fix up all the things in my life that I've messed up, then I'll turn back to You." But God will not be bargained with. You must give up your own way, no strings attached, no conditions, no ifs. But why should that be hard?

Who is it who loves you most? Who has the most invested in your life? Who is it who desires your welfare and your happiness? God Himself, of course! It matters very much to Him that you are happy and that your life is redeemed and made usable again. "If we believe not, yet he abideth faithful: he cannot deny himself," II Timothy 2:13

110

tells us. He promised Himself He'd bring us safely and joy-fully to Heaven (See Heb. 6:18-20).

Are you tired of the past being dredged up again and again? It doesn't have to be that way. "But if the wicked will turn from all his sins that he hath committed, and keep all my statutes, and do that which is lawful and right, he shall surely live, he shall not die. All his transgressions that he hath committed, *they shall not be mentioned unto him:* in his righteousness that he hath done he shall live" (Ezek. 18:21, 22).

Do you need a second chance? God is the God of the second chance. "This is the covenant that I will make with the house of Israel after those days, saith the Lord; I will put my laws into their mind, and write them in their hearts: and I will be to them a God, and they shall be to me a people: For I will be merciful to their unrighteousness, and their sins and their iniquities will I remember no more" (Heb. 8:10, 12).

This God is our God. It is He who offers you a second chance—and a thousand second chances. Why not turn around today and begin to serve Him with all your heart?

appendix I

A Bible-reading schedule for busy women

This system of daily Bible-reading provides a passage from the New Testament for morning reading and a passage from the Old Testament for evening reading. It completes the Bible in one year.

January	New Testament	Old Testament
1	Matthew 1	Genesis 1, 2
2	2	3-5
3	3	6-8
4	4	9-11
5	5:1-20	12-14
6	5:21-48	15-17
7	6:1-18	18, 19
8	6:19-34	20-22
9	7	23, 24
10	8:1-22	25, 26
11	8:23-34	27, 28
12	9	29, 30
13	10:1-23	31, 32

January	New Testament	Old Testament
14	10:24-42	33-35
15	11	36, 37
16	12:1-21	38, 39
17	12:22-50	40, 41
18	13:1-23	42, 43
19	13:24-43	44, 45
20	13:44-58	46-48
21	14	49, 50
22	15:1-28	Exodus 1-3
23	15:29-39	4, 5
24	16	6, 7
25	17	8, 9
26	18	10-12
27	19	13, 14
28	20:1-16	15
29	20:17-34	16, 17
30	21	18, 19
31	22:1-22	20, 21

February	New Testament	Old Testament
1	Matthew 22:23-46	Exodus 22, 23
2	23	24, 25
3	24:1-28	26, 27
4	24:29-51	28
5	25:1-30	29, 30
6	25:31-46	31
7	26:1-30	32, 33
8	26:31-56	34, 35
9	26:57-75	36, 37
10	27:1-26	38, 39
11	27:27-44	40
12	27:45-66	Leviticus 1-3

February	New Testament	Old Testament
13	28	4, 5
14	Acts 1	6, 7
15	2:1-21	8
16	2:22-47	9, 10
17	3	11, 12
18	4	13, 14
19	5:1-15	15
20	5:16-42	16-18
21	6	19-21
22	7:1-29	22
23	7:30-60	23, 24
24	8	25
25	9:1-31	26, 27
26	9:32-43	Numbers 1, 2
27	10:1-23	3, 4
28	10:24-48	5, 6
29	I Corinthians 13	Psalm 19

March	New Testament	Old Testament
1	Acts 11:1-18	Numbers 7, 8
2	11:19-30	9, 10
3	12	11-13
4	13:1-25	14, 15
5	13:26-52	16, 17
6	14	18, 19
7	15:1-21	20, 21
8	15:22-41	22, 23
9	16:1-15	24-26
10	16:16-40	27, 28
11	17:1-15	29-31
12	17:16-34	32, 33
13	18	34-36

March	New Testament	Old Testament
14	19:1-20	Deuteronomy 1, 2
15	19:21-41	3, 4
16	20:1-16	5, 6
17	20:17-38	7-9
18	21:1-16	10-12
19	21:17-40	13-15
20	22:1-16	16-18
21	22:17-30	19-21
22	23	22-24
23	24	25-27
24	25:1-11	28
25	25:12-27	29, 30
26	26:1-18	31, 32
27	26:19-32	33, 34
28	27:1-26	Joshua 1, 2
29	27:27-44	3, 4
30	28:1-16	5-7
31	28:17-31	8, 9

April	New Testament	Old Testament
1	Mark 1:1-20	Joshua 10-12
2	1:21-45	13-15
3	2	16-19
4	3:1-12	20-22
5	3:13-35	23, 24
6	4:1-20	Judges 1, 2
7	4:21-41	3, 4
8	5:1-20	5, 6
9	5:21-43	7, 8
10	6:1-29	9
11	6:30-56	10

April	New Testament	Old Testament
12	7:1-23	11, 12
13	7:24-37	13-15
14	8:1-21	16-18
15	8:22-38	19-21
16	9:1-29	Ruth 1-4
17	9:30-50	I Samuel 1-3
18	10:1-31	4-7
19	10:32-52	8-10
20	11	11-13
21	12:1-27	14, 15
22	12:28-44	16, 17
23	13	18, 19
24	14:1-26	20-22
25	14:27-52	23-25
26	14:53-72	26-28
27	15:1-23	29-31
28	15:24-47	II Samuel 1-3
29	16	4-6
30	Philemon 1	7-9

May	New Testament	Old Testament
1	Romans 1:1-17	II Samuel 10-12
2	1:18-32	13, 14
3	2	15-17
4	3	18, 19
5	4:1-16	20, 21
6	4:17-25	22
7	5	23, 24
8	6:1-14	I Kings 1
9	6:15-23	2, 3
10	7	4-6

May	New Testament	Old Testament
11	8:1-17	7, 8
12	8:18-39	9, 10
13	9	11, 12
14	10	13-15
15	11:1-12	16, 17
16	11:13-36	18, 19
17	12	20, 21
18	13	22
19	14	II Kings 1-3
20	15:1-13	4, 5
21	15:14-33	6, 7
22	16	8, 9
23	I Corinthians 1	10-12
24	2	13-15
25	3	16, 17
26	4	18, 19
27	5	20-22
28	6	23-25
29	7	I Chronicles 1, 2
30	8	3, 4
31	9	5, 6

June	New Testament	Old Testament
1	I Corinthians 10:1-15	I Chronicles 7, 8
2	10:16-33	9, 10
3	11	11-13
4	12	14-16
5	13	17-19
6	14	20-22
7	15:1-34	23-25
8	15:35-58	26-29

June	New Testament	Old Testament
9	16	II Chronicles 1-4
10	II Corinthians 1	5-7
11	2	8-11
12	3	12-15
13	4	16-19
14	5	20-22
15	6, 7	23-25
16	8	26-28
17	9	29, 30
18	10	31, 32
19	11	33, 34
20	12	35, 36
21	13	Ezra 1-4
22	Galatians 1	5, 6
23	2	7, 8
24	3:1-14	9, 10
25	3:15-29	Nehemiah 1-3
26	4:1-20	4-6
27	4:21-31	7
28	5	8-10
29	6	11-13
30	Jude 1	Esther 1, 2

July	New Testament	Old Testament
1	Luke 1:1-25	Esther 3-6
2	1:26-56	7-10
3	1:57-80	Job 1, 2
4	2:1-21	3-5
5	2:22-52	6-8
6	3	9-12

July	New Testament	Old Testament
7	4:1-15	13-15
8	4:16-44	16-19
9	5:1-16	20, 21
10	5:17-39	22-24
11	6:1-19	25-28
12	6:20-49	29-31
13	7:1-29	32-35
14	7:30-50	36-39
15	8:1-21	40-42
16	8:22-39	Psalms 1-6
17	8:40-56	7-10
18	9:1-17	11-16
19	9:18-36	17, 18
20	9:37-62	19
21	10:1-24	20-22
22	10:25-42	23-25
23	11:1-13	26-29
24	11:14-36	30, 31
25	11:37-54	32-34
26	12:1-21	35-37
27	12:22-40	38-41
28	12:41-59	42-44
29	13:1-21	45-48
30	13:22-35	49-51
31	14:1-24	52-55

August	New Testament	Old Testament
1	Luke 14:25-35	Psalms 56-59
2	15	60-63
3	16	64-67
4	17:1-21	68, 69
5	17:22-37	70-72

August	New Testament	Old Testament
6	18	73-75
7	19:1-28	76-78
8	19:29-48	79, 80
9	20:1-26	81-84
10	20:27-47	85-88
11	21	89
12	22:1-30	90-93
13	22:31-53	94-98
14	23:1-26	99-102
15	23:27-38	103, 104
16	23:39-56	105, 106
17	24:1-35	107, 108
18	24:36-53	109-112
19	Ephesians 1:1-14	113-117
20	1:15-23	118-119:40
21	2	119:41-112
22	3	119:113-176
23	4:1-16	120-127
24	4:17-32	128-134
25	5:1-21	135-138
26	5:22-33	139-141
27	6	142-145
28	Philippians 1:1-20	146-150
29	1:21-30	Proverbs 1, 2
30	2	3, 4
31	3	5-7

September	New Testament	Old Testament
1	Philippians 4	Proverbs 8, 9
2	Colossians 1:1-17	10, 11
3	1:18-23	12, 13
4	2	14, 15

A Bible-reading schedule

September	New Testament	Old Testament
5	3	16, 17
6	4	18, 19
7	I Thessalonians 1	20, 21
8	2, 3	22, 23
9	4	24, 25
10	5	26-28
11	II Thessalonians 1	29-31
12	2	Ecclesiastes 1, 2
13	3	3-5
14	I Timothy 1	6-8
15	2	9-12
16	3	Song of Solomon 1, 2
17	4	3-5
18	5	6-8
19	6	Obadiah 1
20	II Timothy 1	Joel 1-3
21	2	Jonah 1-4
22	3	Amos 1-4
23	4	5-9
24	Titus 1	Hosea 1-3
25	2, 3	4-6
26	Hebrews 1	7-9
27	2	10-12
28	3	Isaiah 1, 3
29	4	3-5
30	5	6, 7

October	New Testament	Old Testament
1	Hebrews 6	Isaiah 8, 9
2	7	10-12

October	New Testament	Old Testament
3	8	13, 14
4	9:1-14	15-18
5	9:15-28	19-21
6	10:1-18	22-24
7	10:19-39	25, 26
8	11:1-16	27, 28
9	11:17-40	29, 30
10	12	31, 32
11	13	33, 34
12	James 1	35, 36
13	2	37-39
14	3	40, 41
15	4	42, 43
16	5	44, 45
17	I Peter 1	46, 47
18	2	48, 49
19	3	50, 51
20	4	52, 53
21	5	54, 55
22	II Peter 1	56-58
23	2	59, 60
24	3	61-63
25	John[1] 1:1-18	64-66
26	1:19-51	Micah 1-3
27	2	4, 5
28	3:1-21	6, 7
29	3:22-36	Nahum 1-3
30	4:1-30	Habakkuk 1-3
31	4:31-54	Zephaniah 1-3

[1]The Gospel of John.

November	New Testament	Old Testament
1	Gospel of John 5:1-23	Jeremiah 1, 2
2	5:24-47	3, 4
3	6:1-21	5, 6
4	6:22-40	7, 8
5	7:1-24	9, 10
6	7:25-53	11, 12
7	8:1-11	13, 14
8	8:12-30	15, 16
9	8:31-59	17, 18
10	9:1-17	19-22
11	9:18-41	23-25
12	10:1-18	26-28
13	10:19-42	29, 30
14	11:1-27	31, 32
15	11:28-57	33
16	12:1-19	34, 35
17	12:20-50	36, 37
18	13:1-20	38-40
19	13:21-38	41-43
20	14	44-47
21	15	48, 49
22	16:1-15	50, 51
23	16:16-33	52
24	17	Lamentations 1, 2
25	18	3-5
26	19:1-30	Ezekiel 1, 2
27	19:31-42	3, 4
28	20:1-18	5-7
29	20:19-31	8-10
30	21	11, 12

December	New Testament	Old Testament
1	I John 1	Ezekiel 13-15
2	2	16
3	3	17-19
4	4	20, 21
5	5	22, 23
6	II John 1	24-26
7	III John 1	27, 28
8	Revelation 1	29, 30
9	2:1-17	31, 32
10	2:18-29	33, 34
11	3	35, 36
12	4	37, 38
13	5	39, 40
14	6	41, 42
15	7	43, 44
16	8	45, 46
17	9	47, 48
18	10	Daniel 1, 2
19	11	3, 4
20	12	5, 6
21	13	7, 8
22	14	9, 10
23	15	11, 12
24	16	Haggai 1, 2
25	17	Zechariah 1-3
26	18	4-6
27	19:1-10	7, 8
28	19:11-21	9-11
29	20	12, 13
30	21	Malachi 1, 2
31	22	3, 4

appendix II

*Helpful scriptures
to memorize*

To be sure of salvation

John 1:12, 13
John 3:16-18
John 5:24
John 10:28
Romans 3:10, 23
Romans 5:8
Romans 6:23
Romans 10:9-13
Ephesians 2:8, 9
I John 5:10-13

To deal with sin after salvation

Psalm 38:18
Psalm 51:10
I Corinthians 10:12-14

Hebrews 4:14-16
I John 1:8, 9

To understand the importance of the Bible

Joshua 1:8, 9
Psalm 19:7-14
Psalm 119:9, 11
Matthew 4:4
Matthew 24:35
II Timothy 3:15-17
Hebrews 4:12

To walk the Christian life

Psalm 119:165
Proverbs 15:1
Jeremiah 33:3

To walk the Christian life
Matthew 6:33
Romans 8:28
Romans 12:1, 2
II Corinthians 5:10
Ephesians 4:25-32
Hebrews 11:6
I John 2:15-17

To tell others of Christ
Proverbs 11:30
Mark 5:19
II Corinthians 5:20, 21

To hope in Christ's return
John 14:1-6
Titus 2:11-13
I John 3:2, 3

Bible chapters to memorize
Psalm 23
I Corinthians 13
Romans 8

Index

Index